Anonymous

Latter-day Saints'

Fourth Edition, Part 1 (1894-5)

Anonymous

Latter-day Saints'
Fourth Edition, Part 1 (1894-5)

ISBN/EAN: 9783337337568

Printed in Europe, USA, Canada, Australia, Japan

Cover: Foto ©Lupo / pixelio.de

More available books at **www.hansebooks.com**

LATTER-DAY SAINTS'

YOUNG MEN'S

MUTUAL IMPROVEMENT ASSOCIATIONS

MANUAL.

—PART ONE.—

—[FOURTH EDITION OF FIVE THOUSAND.]—

1894-5.

PUBLISHED BY AUTHORITY.

PRINTED AND FOR SALE BY THE CONTRIBUTOR COMPANY,
SALT LAKE CITY, UTAH.
1894

INTRODUCTION.

THE object of this Manual is to present a practical working aid to the officers and members of the Young Men's Mutual Improvement Associations.

The reasons for following simple and progressive plan and order are obvious from nature's simple formula, viz:—What? How? Why?

The "What is it?" by this time, presumably, is generally understood.

The "How is it to be done?" is of present vital importance; hence the compilation of this Manual.

The "Why is it?" in a general sense, is answered already to those having to do with the associations; in a technical sense it does not so much concern us at present.

It is proposed to issue at a later time, Part II, containing second year's course, and so on till the four years' course is completed. A revision of these four parts can then be made and the whole be bound in a convenient MANUAL as a practical hand-book for the associations.

It is presumed, from the extensive literature published, and personal visits and instructions given, that the officers generally are familiar with the idea of the FOUR BASIC STUDIES, viz:

THEOLOGY,

HISTORY,

SCIENCE,

LITERATURE [see diagram].

All intelligent students will agree that a THEOLOGICAL FOUNDATION is essential, indispensable, imperative.

With a testimony of the Gospel of Christ, the student may safely, successfully and searchingly pursue any and all general or special lines of legitimate thought—pursue with interest with intelligence—with profit—with speed—with profundity—with relation—which relation is truth.

SALT LAKE CITY, UTAH,
July, 1891.

OFFICERS

GENERAL SUPERINTENDENCY.

Superintendent,
WILFORD WOODRUFF.

Counselors,
JOSEPH F. SMITH,
MOSES THATCHER.

Assistants,
JUNIUS F. WELLS,
MILTON H. HARDY,
RODNEY C. BADGER,
GEO. H. BRIMHALL.

Secretary,
GEO. D. PYPER.

Treasurer,
WILLIAM S. BURTON.

Music Director,
EVAN STEPHENS.

GENERAL SUPERINTENDENCY, Y.M.M.I.A.

Salt Lake City, September 1st, 1891.

To the Stake Officers of the Y.M.M.I.A.:

DEAR BRETHREN:—In addressing this our annual letter to you, we take pleasure in introducing this Manual, Part 1, which, under our appointment and direction, has been carefully compiled by Assistant General Superintendent Milton H. Hardy, and Stake Superintendent George H. Brimhall.

You will therefore make it a guide for the year's work, and each one not only become acquainted with, but practically apply the specific instructions addressed to him. In this way, your work, being systematic, will be more progressive and successful than heretofore.

By reference to our former circular letters, you will see the consistency and necessity of our making the following inquiries and suggestions.

How many of your associations began their regular weekly meetings early last year, as suggested?

How many of your officers, stake and ward, secured a set of and became acquainted with the contents of the first year's series, M. I. A. Reading Course, in order to be able to lead in that work this year?

In how many of your associations were music classes organized and conducted according to plan of general music director, as given in current numbers of the *Contributor?*

Have you in each ward in your Stake a Young Men's Mutual Improvement Association?

Is your Stake Superintendency complete?

Did you hold Stake Council Meetings, and prepare for the general work of the stake, for stake officers' meetings, stake conferences, your missionaries, your lectures, stake recreations, and all other matters pertaining to the superintending of the work?

Did you hold Stake Officers' meetings?

Did you hold your half-yearly Stake Conferences?

Did you visit officially each association in your stake twice last year?

Did you examine the records of each association in your stake last year?

Did you make any provisions for public lectures under auspices of the M. I. A. of your wards last year?

Is each association working in harmony with, and recognized as a practical help in each ward?

Did you confer freely and fully with the presidency of your stake in superintending the M. I. A. work last year?

Are you personally acquainted with the educational status and progress of each association in your stake?

Is there a general sentiment in your stake for the officers' to remain faithful to their work until honorably released?

See *Contributor*, Vol. XI., page 471, also inclosed questions with circular letter of March 17, 1891, and ADDRESS, *Contributor*, Vol., IX, pp. 38-40.

It will be well for you to plan for holding your ANNUAL MEETING for sustaining officers in each ward as soon as possible; but the regular weekly meetings should be started up promptly early in September by the present officers, who should not wait for the annual meeting. At the annual meeting it is desirable that the Stake Superintendency should be present. This meeting should be made general in the ward, at which time the importance, plan and purpose of mutual improvement work should be brought clearly and forcibly before the people, and the ward officers sustained by the vote of the Saints. If, for any cause, changes are to be made or vacancies filled, they should be attended to at this meeting.

In the selection of officers the ward authorities should be fully conferred with and great care taken to choose such persons as are fitted for the positions by popularity, ability, and inclination to do the work required.

As will be seen from the Manual, special instructions are given to the members, and each class of officers for their general guidance; to this your attention is directed.

As you are aware, this organization is of such a character that its directing, teaching, training influence extends to the HOME-READING, or preparation of the individual member around the fireside; thence to his regular weekly progressive lesson or exercise; thence

to the monthly joint meeting; thence to the district, and stake conferences and culminating in the general annual conference in June
of each year; thus making the line of organized work practically
complete and progressive.

You are also cognizant of the special importance of regular,
systematic, progressive reading, thinking, and acting on the part of
the individual member; thus permanently impressing and establishing him in this universal system of education, based upon revelation, self-culture, and mutual or associative effort and relation.

Education, as you know, is the development and use of one's
entire self; in other words, the accumulation and proper application
of physical, spiritual, intellectual and moral power; or, the development of correct thought and its expression in righteous words
and actions. (See *Contributor*, Vol. XI., page 351.)

Praying the Lord to preserve, direct and prosper you in your
work of love, we remain your fellow laborers in the cause of Mutual
Improvement.   WILFORD WOODRUFF,
                                JOSEPH F. SMITH,
                                MOSES THATCHER,
                                General Superintendency
                                        Y. M. M. I. A.

Instructions to Superintendents.

The very nature of your office indicates the necessity of your having a personal acquaintance with the status of every association in your Stake.

For special instructions in regard to your duties as superintendents you are cited to the address of the General Superintendency, and also lecture on "Government of the Associations," as published in the *Contributor*, Vol. ix., pp. 257-262.

Now this Manual will aid you in superintending the M. I. A. work in your stake, provided you will make yourselves practically familiar with its contents.

So plan and pursue your stake work that the Manual and the literature referred to will be a necessity in every association. One of the first steps to the accomplishment of this is the immediate calling of your STAKE OFFICERS' meeting, at which the ward officers of every association in your stake should be present. Then, with a copy of this Manual in hand, and one in the hands of each officer present, the work for the entire M. I. year can be so practically laid before them, and the spirit of the work so thoroughly infused, that not only the officers as leaders but the members, as well as the interested public, can plainly see the direct, unbroken line or march of progressive work and exercises, and the year's results can be assured. Since leaders must lead, careful preparation for this and all other stake meetings should be made at stake council meetings.

Having held your stake council meeting, and your stake officers' meetings referred to in the last paragraph, and carefully considered and explained the Manual, emphasizing the instructions to members, to ward officers, and to Stake Superintendents, and finally giving special consideration—PARAGRAPH by PARAGRAPH—to letter of instruction from the General Superintendency, definite arrangements should be made for the beginning of the regular association work in early September, in order that this course may be completed. Although in some instances the attendance at first may be small, this should in no case be made an excuse for delay. The educational character of the associations so plainly seen requires that each year's exercises must have a definite beginning, an uninterrupted continuance, and a termination of practical results as per plan.

In keeping with the instructions of the General Superintendency given last year, so plan early to meet your ward officers' at least four times during the year: that is, once at the Stake Officers' meeting just referred to, once at the annual meeting when you visit them in each ward, once at the Stake Officers' meetings which always precede your half-yearly Stake Conferences and are an essential part of them; as well as conferring with them at your visits that you make during the working year.

The work having been systematically planned and set before the association, the officers should be prepared to give favorable answers to following and other pertinent questions:

How many young men in the ward?

How many are members?

Are ward council or officers' meetings held?

Do they follow regular progressive program from the Manual?

How far have you come in each branch?

Are joint council meetings held to prepare for monthly joint meetings?

Are monthly joint meetings held?

Are the programs for the joint meetings progressive as per instructions to Presidents in the M. I. Manual?

Are public lectures given in your ward under the auspices of the M. I. A.?

To what extent do you lead in the recreation in your ward?*

Have you a M. I. choir?

Is your music class following regular course prepared by our general music director, as published in the *Contributor?*

Do your missionaries fill their appointments, and do the other missionaries visit you regularly?

Is your civil government class progressing intelligently, as per instructions in the Manual?

Have the records of the associations been inspected by Ward Presidents and Stake Superintendents; and do they show history of organization from beginning?

Do the officers all possess a copy of the Manual, and are they following it?

Have the Stake Superintendents a list of all officers and dates of meetings?

Have you following foundation for library:—Complete set of Church works; Bound volumes of *Contributor* complete; Set of M. I. A. Reading Course; Webster's Unabridged Dictionary (International); and a Cyclopedia?

Remark. Questions answered favorably are marked thus, + those unfavorably, thus —, and the list kept for council meetings of the Stake Superintendency.

*See under head of Recreations in this Manual, page 13.

Instructions to Ward Presidents.

1. Make yourselves familiar with the Manual.

2. Assign lessons from it for three successive weekly meetings, with the understanding that officers and members have the Manual, the *Contributor*, the M. I. A. Reading Course, and the four standard works—the Bible, the Book of Mormon, Doctrine and Covenants, and Pearl of Great Price—at least; and that they will prepare their lessons at home. This is what is meant by home-reading or preparation.

3. Distribute the review questions following each subject lectured upon.

4. Each program should be thoughtfully prepared by the president and counselors at the officers' meeting, and should contain a regular lesson for preparation and brief lecture, or report on the following subjects as planned in this Manual:

1. Theology—Gospel—M. I. Series.

2. History
   $\left\{ \begin{array}{l} \text{Bible, O. T.,} \\ \text{Book of Mormon,} \\ \text{New Testament,} \\ \text{Church,} \\ \text{English, M. I. series.} \\ \text{Biographical, M. I. series.} \end{array} \right.$ See Analyses published.

3. Science – First Book of Nature, M. I. Series.

4. Literature
   $\left\{ \begin{array}{l} \text{Readings from Irving, M. I. series.} \\ \text{American Literature.*} \end{array} \right.$

For each program five of these subjects are to be lectured upon, about ten minutes each, and the others reported upon as having been prepared by home-reading; the subjects being taken in succession until a branch of study has been completed. This is what is meant by progressive weekly programs.

---

*This last is for more advanced and for monthly studies only, i. e., one of these studies is given each month. See under head of Literature in this Manual.

To this essential progressive part of the program should be added such refining, recreative exercises as the student can contribute.

Where facilities for conducting special classes in music, civil government, etc., exist, such classes should be organized and directed as part of the association proper. This class-work is conducted by an INSTRUCTOR and the report of attendance and exercises, kept by his class secretary, and reported to the secretary of the association.

For your general guidance and selections in music classes, see instructions and music in the *Contributor*, given by Prof. E. Stephens, general music director. For organization and special direction you will look to your Stake music director.

In organizing and conducting classes in civil government you will be guided by the following:

a. ORGANIZATION.

1. This class as all others is under the general direction of the president of the association of the ward where organized.

2. All members of this class as well as all other classes must be enrolled in the general Roll of the association and each person credited for his attendance and exercises.

3. Sessions of the class should be opened and closed with prayer.

4. In case no one familiar with the principles of civil government can be engaged to instruct the class, then select one of the class for leader and one for secretary.

5. To be eligible to membership in a civil government class the student must be over sixteen years of age.

b. CLASS WORK.

1. Divide the time of the session; one part for political science, and one part for parliamentary law: one hour for each branch. Two or more evenings may be occupied in reading and commenting upon the fundamental principles of law, as set forth by Blackstone, Vol. 1, Sec. 11. For this purpose obtain a copy of Blackstone's Commentaries from your library.

2. Each member having provided himself with a text-book, namely, Townsend's Shorter Course—Civil Government, the class will proceed to consider the subjects in their order, as planned under the head of civil government in this Manual.

3. Townsend's Shorter Course in Civil Government is recommended as a text-book on Political Science; Robert's Rules of Order is recommended as a guide in Parliamentary Law.

4. Consult such other text-books treating upon the subjects given that may be at your disposal.

5. The class furnishes, each week, an exercise for the progressive program of association proper, and each month for the progressive program of the joint meeting.

6. In all matters of public importance, the president of the association is always conferred with.

MONTHLY JOINT MEETINGS.

Programs for these meetings should be carefully made at a monthly joint council meeting of the officers of the Y. M. and Y. L. M. I. associations of the ward, and should contain:

1. Some of the best exercises which have been given in the progressive programs of the regular separate weekly meetings of each association during the month.

2. Short exercises from special classes, as the civil government, music, etc., when organized.

3. Reading of the M. I. Monthly, or joint manuscript paper.

4. This regular progressive part of the monthly program should be supplemented by such refining, recreative general exercises as circumstances may require and determine.   Thus it will be seen that the programs of the Monthly Joint Meetings are also progressive, making the HOME READING, WEEKLY EXERCISES and MONTHLY JOINT MEETINGS all essentially and practically systematic and progressive.

At these joint meetings the president of the Young Men's Association, as presiding officer should confer mutually and fully with the president of the Young Ladies' Association, in conducting the meetings.

Separate rolls should be called and separate minutes taken and made a matter of record, that each association as well as each individual member may receive proper credit for attendance and exercises.

RECORDS AND REPORTS.

Special attention should be given to this branch of the association work.

The minutes of all meetings should be a plain, simple record of the actual business transacted, program as carried out, and summary of attendance.

They should show:

1. Place and time of meeting.

2. Kind of meeting, as officers' regular weekly, monthly joint, or special.

3. Name of young man presiding.
4. What was done and by whom.
5. Members present as shown by roll call.

Minutes of previous meeting should be read for correction and acceptance immediately after opening exercises. They should then be recorded in ink.

The records should be inspected by the ward presidency and stake superintendency, who should see that the history of the association from the time of its organization to date is complete.

All programs should be prepared by the ward presidency at council meetings, and written in the program book. The secretary should keep this book, and before the opening of the meeting he should hand a plain, neat copy of the program to the presiding officer.

While the program is being carried out, the secretary should check off the parts filled, and make them the principal part of his minutes, and then enter these exercises as carried out, in their respective columns in the secretary's summary. (Form No. 2.)

This summary will enable him to show the status of the association at any time, and materially aid him in making out his annual report.

In addition to this summary (Form 2), the secretary will refer to the minutes for following:

1. Number of special or extra meetings.
2. Number of general public lectures.
3. Visits of stake officers.
4. Members on missions.*

All reports should be carefully copied in the record for future reference.

RECREATIONS.

With regard to recreations a reference to the circular letters from the General Superintendency shows it to be your privilege and duty to consider earnestly, manfully and in a business-like manner the providing for, and regulating of, these other and abused divisions of the great M. I. work, particularly the ball-room, the drama, and excursions.

The ball room should be restored to its original school of etiquette and refinement; the drama, to its school of delivery and legitimate delineation; the excursion to the line of legitimate and profitable pleasure under the direction of proper authority.

* This does not refer to the stake or ward inter-missionary work.
Rem.—When a member is sent on a mission it should be so stated opposite his name on the general roll.

Instructions to Members.

You will find this Manual a material aid to you in pursuing the studies of Theology, History, Science, and Literature—the four basic studies.

Being determined to pursue the M. I. Course of study as fast and as far as practicable during the year, you will find the lessons blocked out in each branch in such a manner as to guide you to a completion of a course of instructions, akin to that of an academic education in the special lines of learning herein prescribed.

It will be necessary for you to have, not only a determination to study, but the following text books: Bible, Book of Mormon, Doctrine and Covenants, Pearl of Great Price, Compendium, Set of M. I. Reading Course, the *Contributor*, this Manual and a Dictionary.

In preparing your lessons get control of your intellectual self and concentrate your whole mental energy on one thing at a time. Classify your knowledge and strengthen your memory by self-reviews, and by the proper application of knowledge— which application is wisdom. Remember that you cannot advance with divided attention. So then, to train the mind in concentration of effort is the first element of progress. This and every other step in advancement must be made by divinely directed self-application. This principle is forcibly illustrated in the words of the great Teacher—"Seek and ye shall find," "Knock and it shall be opened unto you." Keep in proper relation with your leaders and associates.

Having accomplished your *preparations through home readings*, attend your meetings with the fixed purpose of giving or receiving something under the direction of the spirit of truth, thus making it pay you by increasing your capacity for usefulness and for the enjoyment of a life of purity and power.

COURSE OF INSTRUCTION.

FIRST YEAR.

·· THEOLOGY. ··

THE GOSPEL.*

LESSON 1.

GENERAL SALVATION.

Subdivisions:—What it is—How made available as a means of salvation to man. Ref. ch. 1 and 2.

Self-review:—1. What is the Gospel? 2. What is salvation?† 3. What is here meant by general salvation? 4. What is here meant by individual salvation? 5. Give three proofs that the resurrection is universal.

LESSON 2.

GENERAL SALVATION, Continued.

Subdivisions:—The Atonement of Christ—Its two-fold force—First from the consequences of Adam's transgression—the redemption as universal as the Fall. Ref. ch. 2, 3 and 4.

Self-review:—1. What is the greatest gift that can be bestowed upon man? 2. What principle was the guiding star of Jesus while on the earth? 3. Show that the great atonement was essential—voluntary—an act of pure love. 4. Name four attributes of Deity made prominent in this lesson. 5. What is secured to all men through the atonement of the Messiah.

LESSON 3.

INDIVIDUAL SALVATION.

Subdivisions:—Redemption from the consequences of personal sins—The principle on which such redemption is based—Brief review of the laws and ordinances to be obeyed. Ref. ch. 5.

---

* This division of Theology is pursued from "The Gospel," M.I. Series, by B. H. Roberts.

† Compendium, page 276, new edition.

Self-review:—1. How far is each individual responsible for the condition of society? 2. On what principle do we all belong to the Redeemer? 3. How is redemption from the consequences of individual sins brought about? 4. What provision is made for those who have died outside of Gospel dispensations? 5. Point out the inconsistency of baptizing infants, and children under eight years of age, i. e., before they arrive at the age of accountability.

Lesson 4.
PRINCIPLES AND ORDINANCES.

Subdivisions:—Faith the first principle of the Gospel—Repentance the second principle of salvation—Baptism principle and ordinance of the Gospel—Confirmation a principle and ordinance—Necessity of accepting the Gospel with all its principles and ordinances—The path of individual progress in the Gospel. Ref. ch. 6.

Self-review:—1. What is meant by an ordinance of the Gospel?* 2. Name ten Gospel ordinances. 3. What qualification is necessary for a man to administer in the ordinances of the Gospel? 4. What is the injunction placed upon those who receive the Gospel? 5. What is necessary to a complete and full salvation?

Lesson 5.
FAITH.

Subdivisions:—What faith is—On what it is based—The importance and necessity of faith in general—In religion—The Being in whom religious faith centers. Ref. ch. 7.

Self-review:—1. What is faith, general? 2. Upon what is general faith based? 3. What is faith as a principle of revealed religion? 4. How can faith be increased? 5. Illustrate the distinction between belief in truth and belief in error.

Lesson 6.
FAITH IN THE BIBLE.

Subdivisions:—Necessity of faith in the Scriptures—They contain the traditions and revelations respecting the existence and character of God—The Bible as a whole. Ref. ch. 8.

Self-review:—1. What is the meaning of the word Bible? 2. By whom were the books of the old Testament collected? 3. Explain the titles, "Old Testament" and "New Testament." 4. Trace the history of the Bible down to its compilation by Ezra. 5. Give three or more reasons for belief in the Bible.

---

*The student is supposed to be familiar with the "Articles of Faith" before passing from the Primary Association.

Lesson 7.

FAITH IN THE OLD TESTAMENT.

Subdivisions.—Faith in the Scriptures—The Old Testament—Authenticity of the books. thereof—The testimony of Josephus—Of the New Testament—The writings of Moses revealed to Joseph Smith—The Book of Abraham—The Book of Mormon. Ref. ch. 8 and 9.

Self-review.—1. Show that whatever evidence supports the Old Testament sustains the New. 2. How does the Pearl of Great Price establish the authenticity of the Old Testament? 3. Prove the authenticity of the Old Testament by the Book of Mormon. 4. Why are Bible readings always refreshing? 5. Mention three of the high literary characteristics of the Bible.

Lesson 8.

FAITH IN THE NEW TESTAMENT.

Subdivisions:—Faith in the Scriptures—The New Testament—The manner in which the collection of its books was made—Authenticity—Credibility. Ref. ch. 10, 11 and 12.

Self-review:—1. Define the word Testament. 2. Give a short account of the compilation of the New Testament. 3. Name in their compiled order the books of the New Testament. 4. Prove the authenticity of the New Testament by the Book of Mormon. 5. How are your feelings affected by the careful perusal of any part of the New Testament?

Lesson 9.

FAITH—TRADITION.

Subdivisions:—The existence of God proved by tradition—How the tradition first came into existence—How preserved—Its universality. Ref. ch. 13.

Self-review:—1. What is tradition? 2. How is tradition a source of faith in God? 3. Where are traces of the ancient patriarchal traditions concerning God to be found? 4. How do the works of nature aid tradition in awakening and fostering faith in a Divine, Supreme Organizer and Director? 5. What is here meant by intelligent belief?

Lesson 10.

FAITH—REVELATION.

Subdivisions:—The existence of God proved by revelation—

2

The revelations of God to Adam, Enoch, brother of Jared, Moses the children of Israel, John the Baptist, the Apostles, Joseph Smith, Sydney Rigdon, Oliver Cowdery.   Ref. ch. 11.

Self-review: –1. Define revelation.   2. Give Scriptural proof that each dispensation of the Gospel has been ushered in by direct revelation.   3. Why has no one a right to deny revelation? 4. Why is regeneration sure to result from a reception of revelation, and degeneracy certain to follow absence or rejection of it?   5. For what purpose and to what extent are all men entitled to direct revelation?

LESSON 11.

FAITH—THE CHARACTER OF GOD.

Subdivisions:—The necessity of knowing something of the attributes of Deity.   1 That He is the supreme governing power of the universe.   2. That He is merciful and slow to anger. 3. Unchangeable.   4. A God of truth.   5. No respecter of persons 6. That He is love. Ref. ch. 15.

Self-review:—1. In addition to faith in the existence of God, what is still needful to the exercise of intelligent faith in His power? 2. Why is faith in God necessarily imperfect without an assurance of His absolute supremacy and perfection?   3. Enumerate the attributes of Deity.   4. Give scriptural evidence that man is in the image of God.   5. How can man become like God?

LESSON 12.

FAITH—COURSE OF LIFE.

Subdivisions:—The course of life essential to the exercise of faith in God –the case of Hezekiah. Ref. ch. 16.

Self-review: –1.   What is the third element of perfect faith in God?   2. Show how faith is weakened by committing that which is wrong or by omitting that which is right, i. e. by sins of commission or omission.   3. Upon what conditions only can eternal life be obtained?   4. How is a knowledge that we are accepted in the sight of God obtained?   5. Name the three elements of perfect faith.

LESSON 13.

REPENTANCE.

Subdivisons:—What it is—Preached by John—Proclaimed by Jesus—Taught by Peter—Effect of repentance and impenitence illustrated by the experience of peoples and nations—Effect of repentance and impenitence illustrated by the experience of individuals. Ref. ch. 17, 18, 19 and 20.

Self-review:—1. What is repentance? 2. Why is repentance logically the second principle of the Gospel? 3. Show that true repentance consists of the following steps: Recognition of wrong in self; desire to make restitution; reformation. 4. Give three historical illustrations of repentance. 5. What is the inevitable destiny of unrepentant nations?

LESSON 14.

BAPTISM.

Subdivisions:—The object of baptism: the remission of sins—The necessity of baptism—Paul's case—Cornelius' case. Ref. ch. 21 and 22.

Self-review:—1. Of what is baptism a type? ·2. Prove that the ordinance of baptism is universal and essential to salvation. 3. What is the object of baptism? 4. What four principles and ordinances of the Gospel must be attended to in order to obtain membership in the Church? 5. Show the obligation of parents in regard to the baptism of their children.

LESSON 15.

SUBJECTS FOR AND MANNER OF BAPTISM.

Subdivisions:—Faith and repentance prerequisites to baptism, hence baptism is for such as are capable of believing and repenting—The folly and sinfulness of infant baptism—The meaning of the verb baptize—Interpretation by the manner in which the servants of Christ baptized. Ref. ch. 22, 23.

Self-review:—1. Prove by divine law and by logic that the baptism of infants and of children under eight years of age is sinful. 2. Narrate the baptism of the Savior. 3. Rehearse the instructions given in the Doctrine and Covenants to be followed in attending to the ordinance of baptism. 4. Why should special attention be paid to cleanliness, and order of immediate surroundings and preparation of subjects at baptisms? 5. Show importance of correct use and recording of names at baptisms and confirmations.

LESSON 16.

THE HOLY GHOST.

Subdivisions: – Gifts thereof free to all who properly seek them

—Who may and who may not obtain the Holy Ghost. Ref. ch. 25, 26.

Self-review:—1. Repeat the words of the Apostle Peter concerning the universality of the promise of the Holy Ghost? 2. How is the Holy Ghost conferred? 3. Show that while every individual may not immediately receive the same special manifestations, yet if the conditions are complied with the promise is sure of fulfillment and the testimony is unmistakable, infallible. 4. Show that purity of thought, words and actions is indispensable to fellowship with the Holy Ghost.

Lesson 17.

THE HOLY GHOST, Continued.

Subdivisons:—How the Holy Ghost is imparted—The laying on of hands—The philosophy of it. Ref. ch. 27.

Self-review:—1. Show that the reception of the Holy Ghost is essential to salvation. 2. Give one complete reference from the New Testament showing manner of bestowing the Holy Ghost. 3. Produce historical evidence substantiating your New Testament proofs. 4. Prove conclusively, by the Doctrine and Covenants that the proper method of conferring the Holy Ghost is by the laying on of hands. 5. Show the vital importance of proper authority and essential expressions of the officer officiating, and complete compliance on the part of the candidate, in order to receive the Holy Ghost.

Lesson 18.

HOLY GHOST, Continued.

Subdivisons:—Character—Source. Ref. ch. 28.

Self-review:—1. Show conclusively the fallacy and blasphemy of the following theory: "We accept as true that only which we can demonstrate." 2. Give New Testament evidence of the source of the Holy Ghost. 3. Give Doctrine and Covenants evidence of the source of the Holy Ghost. 4. Give Doctrine and Covenants evidence of the personality of the Holy Ghost. (Sec. 130, also Lecture 5, Faith.) 5. Show that the light of the Holy Ghost is the only infallible guide to all truth, and that the student who bases his education on this foundation can advance faster and infinitely further in the investigation of truth (see four basic studies) than is possible in any other way.

LESSON 19.

HOLY GHOST—POWER.

Subdivisions:—Teaches all things—Brings all things to remembrance—Shows things to come—Reveals the things of God. Ref. ch. 29.

Self-review:—1. Name four important things learned in this lesson concerning the power of the Holy Ghost. 2. Show that the power of the Holy Ghost is directive, protective, and infinitely progressive in character. 3. Show that prophecy and revelation are and always have been manifestations of the power of the Holy Ghost. 4. Give scriptural evidence that one of the special offices and powers of the Holy Ghost is to testify of Jesus our Redeemer. 5. Show that there are many spiritual gifts by the same power.

LESSON 20.

AUTHORITY.

Subdivisions:—The necessity of possessing divine authority to officiate in things pertaining unto God—To be sent by ligitimate, divinely established authority is to be sent of God—Result of acting without authority. Ref. ch. 30.

Self-review:—1. Give New Testament illustrations of proper authority to administer in the ordinances of the Gospel. 2. How is Divine authority conferred on man? 3. Show the disastrous results of attempting to officiate without authority. 4. Show the imperative necessity of men being properly authorized to officiate and then magnifying their calling 5. Show the chain of authority to administer in the ordinances of the Gospel and to organize the Church of Christ upon the earth.

LESSON 21.

LAWS OF SPIRITUAL DEVELOPMENT.

Subdivisions:—Based upon free and complete acceptance of the principles of salvation in their entirety as revealed—Continuous obedience to and application of the laws and ordinances of the Gospel. Ref. ch. 31.

Self-review:—1. What is meant by spiritual development? 2. Recite in their order the steps of spiritual development as given by Peter. 3. Show that there is no one great thing that man can do and then do no more and obtain eternal life. 4. Show that we must not only be good but actively good. 5. Repeat the instructions of the Prophet Joseph in regard to returning to the presence of our Heavenly Father.

LESSON 22.

HISTORY OF THE GOSPEL.

Subdivisions:—Its antiquity—Its unchangeableness—Historical proofs from the Bible, Pearl of Great Price, New Testament, Doctrine and Covenants, Profane History. Ref. ch. 32.

Self-review:—1. Show that the Gospel as a plan and program of education and salvation antedates the organization of the earth. 2. Prove that man's agency is essential to his salvation. 3. Show that the introduction of the Gospel to Adam was by direct command. 4. Give evidence that the same Gospel in which we believe was taught to Adam. 5. Give New Testament proofs that there is but one Gospel.

LESSON 23.

HISTORY OF THE GOSPEL, Continued.

Subdivisions.—The inseparableness of the Gospel from the Priesthood—Apostasy the cause of the Gospel's being taken from man. Ref. ch. 32.

Self-review:—1. Show that the Priesthood is co-existent with the Gospel, and that exaltation is impossible without it. 2. Explain why the fullness of the Gospel, and with it the holy Melchisedek Priesthood, was taken from ancient Israel. 3. Give evidence of the restoration of the fullness of the Gospel and with it the Melchisedek Priesthood. 4. Show that through apostasy the Gospel was again lost to man. 5. Give proofs of the restoration of the fullness of the Gospel through the Prophet Joseph.

LESSON 24.

SALVATION FOR THE DEAD.

Subdivisions:—The necessity—The Plan—Our practical relationship to the principle. Ref. ch. 33.

Self-review:—1. Relate the circumstances of the restoration of the keys pertaining to the salvation of the dead. (Doc. and Cov., Sec. 110.) 2. Give proofs that the Gospel was preached to the dead by the Messiah. 3. Show that the ordinance of baptism for the dead was administered in the days of the ancient apostles. 4. Explain how the ordinance of baptism for the dead affords us the privilege of officiating as saviors on Mount Zion. 5. Show why we

Lesson 25.
GENERAL REVIEW.

1. Name the principles and ordinances of the Gospel in their order as taught in this book. 2. Give the subdivisional headings under which the subject of faith is treated. 3. Write a short letter to a friend explaining the principle of repentance. 4. Write a ten minutes' lecture on the ordinance of baptism as treated in this book. 5. Formulate five questions on the subject of confirming members of the church. 6. Explain in a ten minutes' summary the source, character and powers of the Holy Ghost. 6. Write in the form of a catechisation, that is, in questions and answers, a five minutes' exercise on Divine Authority (see lesson 20). 8. Prepare a ten minutes' lecture on spiritual development, referring to lesson 21. 9. Give a brief historical sketch of the Gospel, summarizing lessons 22-23. 10. Expound in brief "Salvation for the dead."

HISTORY.

BIBLE—OLD TESTAMENT.

ADAMIC DISPENSATION.

Period B. C. 4004 to 2469.

LECTURE 1.

THE CREATION.

Subdivisions:—Chaotic state of matter—the production of light —Divisions of land and water as comprising the mineral kingdom —Establishing the vegetable kingdom—Establishing the animal kingdom—Introduction of man with authority to exercise dominion over the three other kingdoms. Ref. Gen. 1, 2. Pearl of Great Price. Josephus.

Self-review:—1. What is meant by a dispensation of the Gospel? (See Catechism.) 2. Narrate in their order the steps of the "creation" as recorded in the Bible. 3. Show the beautiful, progressive relationship of the several periods or steps of the "creation." 4. By what authority or right does man stand at the head of, or as ruler over the mineral, the vegetable, and the animal kingdoms of nature? 5. Why was the seventh day designated and set apart as one of special rest and holiness?

LECTURE 2.

ADAM AND EVE IN THE GARDEN OF EDEN.

Subdivisions:—Location of Eden—Description of the garden— The works in the garden—State of innocence and peace. Ref. ch. 2.

Self-review:—1. Where was the Garden of Eden? 2. For what has it ever been celebrated? 3. What provision was made for the care of the garden? 4. What is the origin of the natural history nomenclature? 5. Show that the garden was a place of intelligent activity and not one of mere passive existence. 6. What was the first great commandment?

LECTURE 3.

THE FALL.

Subdivisions:—The Tempter - Disobedience—The remorse of conscience—The vain excuses—The banishment. Ref. Gen. 3.

Self-review:—1. What is meant by the "Fall?" 2. Who was the tempter? 3. Why were Adam and his wife banished from the garden? 4. What was the object of guarding the way to the "Tree of Life?" 5. What is meant by remorse of conscience?

LECTURE 4.

CAIN AND ABEL.

Subdivisions:—Their dispositions—Their occupations—Causes of their disagreement—Cain's evil adviser - Abel's obedience to his parents—The sacrifice—The murder. Ref. Gen. 4., Pearl of Great Price.

Self-review:—1. What occupations did Cain and Abel follow respectively? 2. What was the apparent cause of their disagreement? 3. What was the real cause of their disagreement? (See Pearl of Great Price.) 4. What was the result of their disagreement? 5 What protection was provided for Cain after the murder and sentence?

LECTURE 5.

ENOCH.

Subdivisions:—His relationship to Adam—Condition of society in his youth—His mission. Time 2948 B. C. Ref. Gen. 5. Pearl of Great Price.

Self-review:—1. Who was Enoch? 2. For what has he ever been justly famed? 3. What became of Enoch, his people, and city? 4. What eternal principle is illustrated in the life of Enoch and his people. 5. What is meant by the Order of Enoch?

LECTURE 6.

THE TEN PATRIARCHS.

Adam—Seth—Enos— Cainan — Mahalaleel — Jared—Enoch—Methuselah—Lamech—Noah. Ref. Gen. 5.

Self-review:—1. Among these ten patriarchs who have received the greatest prominence? 2. How was Enoch related to both Adam and Noah? 3. What was the average age of these great men? 4. What was the form of government during this period? 5 How many of these patriarchs were contemporary? 6. In what part of the earth did they all reside?

NOACHIAN DISPENSATION.

Time B. C. 2348 to 1922.

LECTURE 7.

THE DELUGE.

Subdivisions.—The necessity—The preparation—The manner —The significance—The result. Ref. Gen. 7 and 8.

Self-review:—1. Of what is the Deluge typical? 2. What was the social condition at the time of the deluge? 3. What preparation had been made for the deluge? 4. What special covenant did God establish with Noah immediately after the flood? 5. What *authority* and *commandment* were repeated to Noah, that were given in the Adamic Dispensation?

LECTURE 8.

HAM'S SIN AND CURSE.

Subdivisions.—His previous disobedience—His merited punishment—The nature and effects of the punishment. Time B. C. 2347. Ref. Gen. 9.

Self-review:—1. Wherein lay the foundation for Ham's condemnation? 2. How did Ham differ from his brothers, Shem and Japheth, regarding filial affection? 3. What was the nature of Ham's punishment? 4. What effects of this punishment are now to be seen? 5. What part of the earth is principally inhabited by the descendants of Ham?

LECTURE 9.

THE TOWER OF BABEL.

The object of building it—The construction—The result. Time B. C. 2247. Ref. Gen. 11.

Self-review:—1. What is said of the universality of the language at the time of building the Tower? 2. What is the meaning of the word Babel? 3. Where was the Tower built? 4. What was the object assigned in building the Tower? 5. What results do we see today of the confusion of the universal language?

ABRAHAMIC DISPENSATION.

Period B. C 1922 to 1491.

LECTURE 10.

ABRAHAM.

Subdivisions:—Ancestry of Abraham—Calling of Abraham—Abraham and Lot—Abraham and Melchisedek. Ref. Gen. 12, Pearl of Great Price, and Compendium Gems.

Self-review:—1. Where is Chaldea? 2. Why did Abraham leave his home? 3. Repeat the word of the Lord to Abraham relative to leaving his country and kindred. 4. Who accompanied Abraham on this journey? 5. Where is the land of Canaan? 6. To whom did Abraham pay tithes?

LECTURE 11.

GOD'S PROMISE TO ABRAHAM.

Subdivisions:—Nature of the promise—The visit of the three angels. Time B. C. 1913. Ref. Gen. 17 and 18.

Self-review:—1. What great promise did God make to Abraham? 2. Why were the names of Abram and Sarai changed to Abraham and Sarah? 3. Why did the Lord place such great confidence in Abraham (See Pearl of Great Price)? 4. What was the special errand of the three heavenly messengers? 5. Why did Abraham plead for the sparing of the cities, the sites of which are now supposed to be covered with the Dead Sea?

LECTURE 12.

ABRAHAM AND ISAAC.

Subdivisions:—Birth of Isaac—Offering of Isaac—Marriage of Isaac—Death and burial of Abraham. Time B. C. 1896 to 1831. Ref. Gen. 21 to 25.

Self-review:—1. What was the promise to Abraham concerning Israel? 2. Repeat the promise made to Abraham immediately following his perfect obedience relative to the offering of his son. 3. What special vow was required by Abraham concerning the marriage of Isaac? 4. Show that Rebekah, Isaac's wife, was selected by inspiration. 5. Where and by whom was Abraham buried?

ESAU AND JACOB.

Subdivisions:—Their occupation—Their respective estimation of the value of the sacred birthright—The alien marriage of Esau—His revengeful feelings concerning Jacob. Time B. C. 1760 to 1736. Ref. Gen. 25 to 27.

Self-review:—1. What were the distinctive characteristics between Esau and Jacob? 2. Why did Esau treat his birthright so indifferently? 3. What were the special distinctions between the blessings received by the two boys? 4. What was the real cause of Esau's hatred toward Jacob? 5. Show that the blessing of Abraham was conferred upon Jacob.

LECTURE 14.

JACOB AT BETHEL.

Subdivisions:—His dream—His tithe covenant. Time B. C. 1760. Ref. Gen. 28.

Self-review:—1. Where is Bethel? 2. What was the cause of Jacob's being at Bethel? 3. What did Jacob dream at Bethel? 4. What covenant did Jacob make at Bethel? 5. What blessing was given to Jacob at Bethel?

LECTURE 15.

JACOB AND HIS TWELVE SONS.

Subdivisions:—His marriage—His prosperous sojourn with Laban—His family. Time B. C. 1728. Ref. Gen. 28 to 35.

Self-review:—1. What sacred injunction was placed upon Jacob by his parents in regard to his marriage? 2. Show the direct relation between Jacob's remarkable financial prosperity and his sacred keeping of the Tithe Covenant. 3. Name the twelve sons of Jacob, the patriarch and prince. 4. Why was Jacob's name changed to Israel? 5. What blessing was bestowed upon Jacob on his return to Bethel?

LECTURE 16.

JOSEPH IN EGYPT.

Subdivisions:—Cause of his being in Egypt—His temptation and victory—His gift as a revelator—His promotion to governorship thereby becoming a savior to his father's house. Time B. C. 1728 to 1706. Ref. Gen. 37, 39, 40.

Self-review.—1. What circumstance brought Joseph into Egypt? 2. Mention two noble thoughts or inspirations that protected Joseph in the hour of temptation. 3. In what instances especially did Joseph exercise the gift of a revelator during his imprisonment? 4. What was the extent of Joseph's civil authority in Egypt? 5. How did Joseph become a savior to his father's house?

LECTURE 17.

JOSEPH'S ADMINISTRATION AS GOVERNOR IN EGYPT.

Subdivisions:—His plan for storing and disposing of grain— His providing for his father's house—Death and burial of his father, Jacob. Time B. C. 1688. Ref. Gen. 41–50.

Self-review:—1. What plan was adopted by Joseph for collecting and distributing grain? 2. What was the result of Joseph's financial administration? 3. What dream of Joseph's was literally fulfilled when his brothers came down from Egypt for corn? 4. What was the numerical strength of Israel at the time they came into Goshen? 5. Why was the land of Goshen given to the Israelites?

MOSAIC AND PROPHETIC DISPENSATION.

Time B. C. 1491 to 397.

LECTURE 18.

EARLY LIFE OF MOSES.

Subdivsions:—His parentage - His typical name—His princely education—His military career—His marriage with the princess of Ethiopia—His flight to Midian—His chivalrous defense of the daughters of Reuel. Time B. C. 1571. Ref. Ex. 2. Also Josephus, book 2, ch. 10, 11.

Self-review:—1. What is the meaning of the word Moses? 2. What was the political condition of Israel at the time of the birth of Moses? 3. Where was Moses educated? 4. Give two illustrations of the valor of Moses. 5. Why did the children of Israel desire to leave the land of Goshen?

LECTURE 19.

COMMISSION OF MOSES.

Subdivisions:—The burning bush on Mount Horeb—The message of the Great I Am—Moses' meekness—The rod of power— Moses' journey to Egypt—Moses and Aaron. Time B. C. 1491. Ref. Ex. 3, 4.

Self-review:—1. Where is Mount Horeb? 2. What special message did Moses receive there? 3. What plea did Moses interpose on Mount Horeb in relation to his ability to perform his mission? 4. How did the Lord convince Moses of His power? 5. Who was sent with Moses as his spokesman?

LECTURE 20.

PREPARATION FOR ISRAEL'S RELEASE FROM BONDAGE.

Subdivisions:—The Elders' conference—The official message to Pharoah—The increased tasks—The crushed spirit of the Israelites—Jehovah's renewed covenants respecting Israel—Moses' unheeded counsels. Time B. C. 1491. Ref. Ex. 4, 5, 6.

Self-review:—1. What conference was held on Moses' return to Egypt? 2. What divine message did Moses bear to Pharaoh? 3. What was the result of Moses' first demand for the release of Israel? 4. Whom did the children of Israel blame for their increased burdens? 5. What covenant was renewed to Israel?

LECTURE 21.

THE TEN PLAGUES.

Subdivisions:—The superiority of God's power over that of the sorcerers'—The waters changed into blood—The plagues of frogs and lice baffling the enchanters—The fly plagues favoring Goshen —The cattle disease—The boil affliction disabling the magicians— The hail storm with great electric phenomenon—The locusts—The darkness—The smiting of the first-born of Egypt. Ref. Ex. 9, 12.

Self-review:—1. How was the superiority of God's power over that of the sorcerers' shown? 2. Name in their order the ten plagues. 3. What explanation is given for the repeated hardening of Pharaoh's heart? 5. Tell how the plagues were stopped among the Egyptians.

LECTURE 22.

THE PASSOVER.

Subdivisions:—Nature of the ordinance—Conditions required for its observance —Duration of the feast—Result of its observance. Time B. C. 1491. Ref. Ex. 12. Josephus, Book II, ch. 14-15.

Self-review:—1. What is meant by the Passover? 2. What is unleavened bread? 3. How many days does the feast of the Passover last? 4. What is the object of the feast of the Passover? 5. What was the result of the observance of the first Passover?

LECTURE 23.

THE DEPARTURE FROM EGYPT.

Subdivisions:—The route taken—The encampment by the Red

Sea—Pharoah and his haughty hosts—Murmurings of the Hebrews
—The fidelity of Moses—Passage through the Red Sea—The two
typical miracles: (a) Manna, (b) Water from the rock—Supporting
the Prophet's arms during the battle of Rephidim—Arrival at
Sinai. Time, 1491 B. C. Ref. Ex. 13 to 18. Josephus Book II,
ch. 15, 16.

Self-review:—1. Why did not the Israelites take the most direct
route for Canaan? 2. By what were the people guided through
the wilderness? 3. Describe the place where Israel camped near
the Red Sea? 4. How did the Israelites cross the Red Sea?
5. Describe the manna provided for the children of Israel.

LECTURE 24.
ISRAEL'S SOJOURN AT SINAI.

Subdivisions:—Visit of Jethro, priest of Midian, (a) the object
of his visit, (b) his wise counsel in regard to organization and
government—Moses on Mount Sinai –The Ten Commandments—
The divers laws and ordinances for Israel—Revelation to Moses—
Opening of the heavens to Moses, Aaron, Nadab, and Abihu, and
seventy of the elders of Israel—The portable tabernacle and ark—
Special setting apart of Aaron and his sons to the Aaronic or
Levitical priesthood—The idolatry of the people in the absence of
their prophet—The two tables of testimony and the two tables of
stone. Time, 1491. B. C. Ref. Ex. 18-34. Josephus, Book III,
ch. 3-8.

Self-review:—1. What was the object of Jethro's visit to the
camp of Israel? 2. Repeat the Ten Commandments. 3. To whom
was the heavens opened at Sinai? 4. Give a general description of
the portable tabernacle. 5. To which priesthood were Aaron and
his sons set apart?

LECTURE 25.
MOSAIC LAWS.

Subdivisions:—Liberality of the people in donating for the
tabernacle. See Ex. 35-60. Josephus Book III. chapter 6-7.
Offerings—Burnt, Peace, Trespass—Law in relation to meats –
Feasts. Time, 1491 B. C. Ref. Book of Leviticus. Josephus
Book III, ch. 9-12.

Self-review:—1. How were the means obtained for the building
of the tabernacle? 2. Name three kinds of offerings instituted.
3. What law was given in relation to the use of meats? 4. What
feasts were instituted among the Israelites? 5. What was the pen-
alty for unchastity among the Israelites?

BOOK OF MORMON.

NEPHITIC DISPENSATION.

Period, B. C. 600 to 421 A. D.   Asia—America.

LECTURE 1.

INTRODUCTION.

Subdivisions:—The title of the Book of Mormon—What the book is—Its origin—By whom written—How preserved—When and by whom brought forth—How translated—The Three Witnesses—The Eight Witnesses—Its coming forth a literal fulfillment of prophecy(Is. xxix). Ref. Preface to Book of Mormon.

Self-review:—1. What is the Book of Mormon? (Comp. p. 312.) 2. What was the origin of the Book of Mormon? 3. By whom was the Book of Mormon originally written? 4. How was the record from which the Book of Mormon was translated preserved? 5. What angel had special charge of the plates containing the Book of Mormon, and delivered them to Joseph Smith? 6. Describe the plates of gold from which the Book of Mormon was translated.* (Answers to Questions, p. 38. Life of Joseph Smith p. 49.) 7. When were the plates delivered to Joseph? (Pearl of Great Price, p. 67.) 8. How was the Book of Mormon translated? (Pearl of Great Price, p. 69.) 9. Name the eleven witnesses to the Book of Mormon. 10. What ancient prophecy was literally fulfilled by the coming forth of the Book of Mormon? (Is. xxix. II Nephi, 27.)

LECTURE 2.

LEHI'S VISION.

Subdivisions.—Social condition of the Jews—Warning prophets —Lehi's earnest pleadings for the people—The pillar of fire—The throne of God—The Messiah and the Twelve Apostles—Reading of the book—Lehi's devotional utterances—His preaching and and prophesying to the people—The people's mockings and persecu-

---

* Each plate was six inches wide, eight inches long, and a little thinner than common tin, and the whole bound together, as the leaves of a book, with three rings. The entire volume was about six inches in thickness. Part of it was sealed.

tions—Leaving Jerusalem in obedience to the command of the Lord—The sojourn in the valley of Lemuel—Murmurings of Laman and Lemuel—Direct revelation in answer to Nephi's prayer. Time 600 B. C. Ref. 1 Nephi, 1 and 2.

Self-review:—1. In what year was Lehi's vision given? 2. What was the social condition of the Jews at that time? 3. How did the people receive the teachings of Lehi? 4. What was the cause of Lehi's leaving Jerusalem? 5. What method did Nephi adopt for obtaining information concerning his course in life? 6. What calamity came upon Jerusalem ten years after he left it, as predicted by Lehi?* 7. Why did Laman and Lemuel find fault and oppose their father from the beginning?

Lecture. 3.

RETURN OF NEPHI AND HIS BROTHERS TO JERUSALEM FOR THE RECORDS.

Subdivisions:—Father Lehi commanded to send for the records —Faith, respect, and obedience of Nephi in contrast to the doubt, disrespect, and opposition of Laman and Lemuel—The consultation and casting of lots—Laman's failure and Nephi's faith and determination to succeed—The coercive measures of Laman and Lemuel —The interference of the angel—Rejection of the testimony of the angel by Laman and Lemuel—Nephi's scriptural exhortation — Nephi's success in obtaining the records that rightly belonged to the family. Ref. I Nephi, 3, 4,

Self-review—1. What was the special object of obtaining the records? 2. Contrast Nephi's faith, respect, and obedience with the doubt, disrespect and opposition of Laman and Lemuel. 3. What was Nephi's memorable and inspirational response when he was asked by his father if he would fulfill the commandment of the Lord in returning to Jerusalem for the records? 4. How was Nephi protected from the cruelty of his brothers? 5. Show that doubt will reject even the testimony of an angel.

Lecture 4.

NEPHI'S SECOND JOURNEY TO JERUSALEM.

Subdivisions:—Ishmael's family—Rebellion in the wilderness— The sacrifice and burnt offerings in the wilderness. Time, 600 B. C. Ref. I Nephi, 7.

---

* Jerusalem was destroyed and the inhabitants taken captive by the Babylonian King, Nebuchadnezzar. (Bible and Josephus.)

Self-review:—1. Why did Nephi return to Jerusalem the second time? 2. Of whom did Ishmael's family consist? 3. What rebellion took place in the wilderness? 4. How was Nephi freed from his bands during the rebellion in the wilderness? 5. What spirit did Nephi manifest toward his brethren after his deliverance? 6. What sacred ordinance was performed on the return of Nephi and his brethren?

LECTURE 5.

LEHI'S DREAM.

Subdivisions:—The man in the white robes—The tree—The river—The rod of iron—The spacious building.   Time, 600 B. C. Ref. I Nephi, 8-11.

Self-review:—1. What was meant by "the man in the white robes?" 2. What was the meaning of the "tree?" 3. What did the "river" represent? 4. Of what was the "rod of iron" a representation? 5. Of what was the "spacious building" illustrative?

LECTURE 6.

LEHI'S PROPHECY.

Subdivisions:—The destruction of Jerusalem—The Messiah— John the Baptist—The baptism of Christ in Jordan—The crucifixion and resurrection of Jesus—The land of promise—The scattering of the Jews—The Gospel to the Gentiles.   Time, 600 B. C. Ref. I Nephi, 10.

Self-review:—1. What did Lehi prophesy in the wilderness concerning Jerusalem? 2. What was his prophetic declaration concerning the Messiah and His forerunner? 3. What did he declare concerning the Gentiles? 4. What did he testify concerning the scattering and gathering of the Jews? 5. What was his testimony concerning the Land of Promise?

LECTURE 7.

NEPHI'S VISION.

Subdivisions:—The Virgin Mary—The Twelve Apostles of Jesus —The internecine war between the Nephites and the Lamanites— The destruction of the Nephites—The dwindling of the Lamanites —The nations of Europe—The Catholic church—The Atlantic ocean—The navigator, Columbus—The Pilgrim Fathers—The American colonies—The oppression of the Indians—The Revolutionary War—The U. S. government—The Bible—The preservation of the Indians—The Book of Mormon, Doctrine and Covenants and other records—the two churches—John the Revelator. Ref.: I Nephi, 11, 12, 14,.

Self-review:—1. What was Nephi's special desire preceding this vision? 2. Show that righteous desire and perfect belief are stepping stones to revelation. 3. What dream and prophecies were made known to Nephi through his vision? 4. Why was Nephi forbidden to write his entire vision? 5. What final triumph yet in store for the Lamanites was shown to Nephi?

LECTURE 8.

THE BALL AND DIRECTOR.

Subdivisions:—Description—Use—Guidance to temporary home at Shazar—The broken bow—The murmurings—The reproof on the ball. Ref. I Nephi, 16.

Self-review:—1. What was the ball and director? (Story of the Book of Mormon, p. 43) 2. In which part of the land did the ball and director lead Nephi? 3. How did Nephi replace his steel bow? 4. How did Nephi receive information concerning the obtaining of food? 5. What serious difficulties followed the death of Ishmael?

LECTURE 9.

THE SOJOURN IN BOUNTIFUL. (Arabia Felix.)

Subdivisions:—Southward journey to it—Its locality—Its natural resources—Nephi's revelation—Preparation for the voyage to the promised land (America). Time B. C. 592. Ref. I Nephi, 17.

Self-review:—1. Where was the land Bountiful? 2. Name two of the natural resources of the country. 3. What revelation did Nephi receive there? 4. Who superintended the building of the ship? 5. How did the ship differ from ordinary vessels?

LECTURE 10.

THE OCEAN JOURNEY.

Subdivisions:—The departure, about twenty degrees north latitude—The storm at sea—The landing in Chili, South America, about thirty degrees south latitude. Time 590 B. C. Ref. I. Nephi, 18.

Self-review:—1. What was the point of departure from Arabia? 2. What was the first event of importance that transpired on the voyage? 3. What infamous treatment was Nephi subjected to? 4. Locate on the map the point of landing. 5. What natural resources did they immediately discover? 6. What immediate provision was made for the continuation of the records after the landing?

LECTURE 11.
DEATH OF LEHI.

Subdivisions:—The circumstances—The immediate division of the family—Origin of the two nations. Ref. II Nephi, 4-5.

Self-review:—1. To whom did Lehi give special individual instructions before his death? 2. In his instructions to his son Joseph, which prophecies given by Joseph who was sold into Egypt and which have been fulfilled, did Lehi repeat? 3. Immediately following the death of Lehi, what did Laman and Lemuel plan to do with Nephi? 4. How did Nephi escape from the murderous designs of his brethren? 5. What two great nations had their origin in this separation of the family?

LECTURE 12.
THE FIRST NEPHITE TEMPLE.

Subdivisions:—Plan of construction—Obvious objects of building it—Jacob and Joseph consecrated priests to officiate among the people. Time, 571 B. C. Ref. II Nephi, 5.

Self-review:—1. What was the plan of this Nephite Temple? 2. What was the obvious object in building it? 3. To what special labor were Jacob and Joseph consecrated? 4. When was this Temple built? 5. What was the general direction taken by Nephi and his people after the separation?

LECTURE 13.
LAMAN'S CURSE.

Subdivisions:—Causes that led to the curse—Effects of the curse. Time 570 B. C. Ref. II Nephi 5.

Self-review:—1. What was the nature of the curse of Laman? 2. What was the cause of it? 3. What was the object of it? 4. What are the visible effects of this curse today? 5. Cite an instance where this curse has been removed. (III Nephi, 2.)

LECTURE 14.
JACOB THE RECORDER.

Subdivisions:—His zealous disposition—His calling as a High Priest—His labors as a recorder. Time, 545 B. C. Ref. Jacob, 1.

Self-review:—1. Which plates were given into Jacob's charge? 2. What class of matter only could be written upon these plates? 3. What form of government was adopted on the death of Nephi? 4. Why did the Nephites keep two sets of records? 5. What were Jacob's and Joseph's views with regard to diligence in office?

LECTURE 15.

SHEREM THE ANTI-CHRIST.

Subdivisions:—The hypocritical questions to Jacob—The sign-seeking—The confession of the impostor. Time, 545 B. C. Ref. Jacob 7. *Contributor,* Vol. 2.

Self-review:—1. What is meant by the term, "Anti-Christ?" 2. In what did Sherem profess to believe? 3. How did Jacob prove to Sherem that he could not believe the Scriptures and at the same time deny the Christ? 4. What was the result of Sherem's blasphemous demand for a sign? 5. To what did Sherem confess before his death?

LECTURE 16.

ENOS AND JAROM.

Subdivisions:—The worldly-mindedness of the people—The continual warning of the church authorities—The wars with the Lamanites. Time, 401 to 362 B. C. Ref. Books of Enos and Jarom. (Story of the Book of Mormon, pp. 68-71.)

Self-review:—1. How did Enos receive a testimony of the forgiveness of his sins? 2. What covenant did the Lord make with him concerning the preservation and bringing forth of the records? 3. What was the condition of the Lamanites in the days of Enos? 4. What was the social and religious tendency of the people in the days of Jarom? 5. Which class of officers was laboring diligently for the reformation of the people?

LECTURE 17.

DISCOVERY OF ZARAHEMLA BY MOSIAH.

Subdivisions:—Cause of Mosiah's leaving his people—The journey toward the isthmus—The meeting with the people of Zarahemla—Their illiterate, infidel condition—Their mutual improvement under Mosiah's system of education—Their union with the people of Mosiah—The account in stone of Coriantumr, the Jaredite, Ref. Omni, 1.

Self-review:—1. What led to the discovery of Zarahemla by Mosiah? (Story of the Book of Mormon, p. 72) 2. Where was the land of Zarahemla? 3. Who were the Zarahemlaites? 4. What was the educational status of the Zarahemlaites? 5. What system of mutual improvement did Mosiah establish among the Zarahemlaites? 6. Who was Coriantumr?

LECTURE 18.
KING BENJAMIN'S ADMINISTRATION.

Subdivisions:—The unauthorized attempts of his subjects to possess the land of Nephi—The transfer of the records from the recorder, Amaleki, to the king—The special training of the three sons of King Benjamin—The conferring of the official trusts upon Mosiah—The calling of a special conference—Mosiah, the son of Benjamin, proclaimed king—King Benjamin's discourse. Ref. Mosiah, 1. (Story of the Book of Mormon, ch. 10.)

Self-review:—1. What was the result of the unauthorized attempt made by some of the people to repossess the land of Nephi? 2. What was the character of the education of the three sons of King Benjamin? 3. What was the object and end of the special conference called by King Benjamin? 4. By what authority was Mosiah proclaimed king? 5. What arrangements were made for the people to hear the discourse of the Prophet-King Benjamin?

LECTURE 19.
ADMINISTRATION OF KING MOSIAH, SON OF BENJAMIN.

Subdivisions:—The farmer king—The Lehi-Nephi searching party—Meeting with King Limhi, the Zarahemlaite—Ammon's historical address—The twenty-four gold plates and ancient armor. Time, 124 B. C. Ref. Mosiah, 6 to 8.

Self-review:—1. What was the occupation of King Mosiah? 2. What was the purpose of sending the searching party of sixteen men back to the land of Nephi? 3. Who was King Limhi? 4. Why was King Limhi so pleased to hear from the Nephites in Zarahemla? 5. Where were the twenty-four gold plates found, and what did they contain?

LECTURE 20.
ADMINISTRATION OF KING MOSIAH, Continued.

Subdivisions:—Zeniff's record—Noah, the king, and Abinadi the prophet—Alma and the waters of Mormon—Gideon and Limhi—Ammon the leader out of bondage. Ref. Mosiah, 9 to 22.

Self-review:—1. What does the record of Zeniff contain? 2. What prophecy was literally fulfilled in the death of King Noah? 3. What was the mission of Abinadi the prophet? 4. Show that the martyrdom of Abinadi was the result of priestcraft, as was the crucifixion of the Savior and the assassination of Joseph the prophet? (Story of the Book of Mormon, ch. 12.) 5. Why were King Limhi and the converted of his people not baptized during the time of Ammon?

LECTURE 21.

ADMINISTRATION OF KING MOSIAH, Continued.

Subdivisions:—Alma and his people—The flight to Helam— The captivity—Popular education among the Lamanites—Amulon the petty tyrant—The miraculous easing of burdens and deliverance of the people of Alma—The union with the people of Mosiah. Ref. Mosiah, 23–25.

Self-review:—1. What form of government was adopted by the people of Alma? 2. How were the people of Alma delivered from bondage? 3. What provision was made for the general education of the Lamanites at this time? 4. What was the condition of the people of Alma just previous to their final deliverance? 5. By what means was the army of the Lamanites prevented from overtaking the people of Alma during their twelve days' journey to Zarahemla? 6. To what office was Alma appointed after the union of his people with the people of Mosiah in Zarahemla? 7. What was the object of having the records read?

LECTURE 22.

THE NEPHITIC JUDGESHIP.

Subdivisions:—The new form of government—The Nephite republic—Alma, the first chief judge. Time, 91 B. C. Ref. Mosiah, 29. (Story of the Book of Mormon, ch. 23.)

Self-review:—1. Who was the last Nephite king? 2. What form of government was adopted at the death of Mosiah? 3. In what year was the Nephite Republic established? 4. Who was the first chief judge of the Nephitic Republic? 5. Explain the departments of government in the Nephite Republic.

LECTURE 23.

PRIESTCRAFT AND APOSTASY.

Subdivisions:—Nehor, the murderer, and Gideon, the martyr— Spread of priestcraft—Class distinctions among dissenters—Fraternity among the faithful. Ref. Alma, 1.

Self-review:—1. What was the first recorded case of capital punishment in the new government? 2. Show that the laws protected every man in his belief. 3. What was the social condition during the first and second years of the republic? 4. Which class of people was inclined to persecute others. 5. Which class of citizens of the republic provided for the poor and needy?

LECTURE 24.

THE CIVIL WAR.

Subdivisions:—Amlici, the rebel—Battles of Sidon River—The alliance of the Amlicites with the Lamanites—The hand-to-hand contest between the chief commanding officers. Time, 81 B. C. Ref. Alma, 2–4.

Self-review:—1. What was the cause of the first civil war of the republic? 2. Name the first great battle of this war. 3. What was the name of the rebel faction? 4. What prophecy of Nephi did the rebels unwittingly fulfill in marking themselves for battle? 5. What was the result of the war?

LECTURE 25.

REIGN OF THE JUDGES.

Subdivisions:—Peace—Industry—Prosperity—Pride—Misuse of accumulated wealth—Alma's resignation of the judgeship, and appointment of Nephihah—Alma's preaching tour, beginning at Zarahemla. Ref. Alma, 2–5.

Self review:—1. How long did Alma serve as chief judge? 2. Who succeeded Judge Alma in the chief judgeship? 3. Why did Judge Alma resign? 4. Show that Alma esteemed his duties in the priesthood far above the highest political position? 5. What steps did Alma take to bring about a reformation among the people?

NEW TESTAMENT.

DISPENSATION OF THE MERIDIAN OF TIME.

Period, 1 *B. C. to* 97 *A. D.*

LECTURE 1.

THE ANNUNCIATION OF JOHN THE BAPTIST.

Subdivisions:— Parentage — Circumstances — The messenger, Gabriel. Ref. Luke 1.

Self-review:—1. What was the special calling of John's father? 2. What is meant by the "Annunciation?" 3. What was the promise of the angel to Zacharias? 4. What was the name of the messenger who announced John the Baptist? 5. What was the result of Zacharias' disbelief?

LECTURE 2.

ANNUNCIATION OF JESUS.

Subdivisions:—Gabriel's mission to Nazareth—The salutation— The relation of Mary to Elizabeth—The prophetic meeting of Mary and Elizabeth. Ref. Luke 1.

Self-review:—1. Give the location of Nazareth. 2. What was Gabriel's mission to Nazareth? 3. Contrast the faith of Mary with the doubt of Zacharias. 4. What were the ties of consanguinity between Mary the mother of Jesus and Elizabeth the mother of John? 5. Of what lineage was Joseph, the husband of Mary?

LECTURE 3.

BIRTH OF JOHN THE BAPTIST.

Subdivisions:—Birthplace—His revealed name—His father's prophecy. Ref. Luke 1.

Self-review:—1. Indicate on your Bible map Hebron the birthplace of John the Baptist. 2. Why was this great prophet named John? 3. What is the meaning of the word John? 4. What was

Zacharias' prophecy concerning his son John?   5. What were the surroundings of John during his childhood?

LECTURE 4.

BIRTH OF CHRIST.

Subdivisions.—The predicted birthplace—The journey of Joseph and Mary from Nazareth to Bethlehem—The object—The results. Ref. Luke 2.

Self-review:—1. Describe the location of Bethlehem? 2. What political movement brought Joseph and Mary from Nazareth to Bethlehem? 3. What was their mode of traveling? 4. What ancient prophecy was fulfilled by Joseph and his wife's going to Bethlehem? (Micah v, 2.) 5. Explain the immediate cause of their humbly lodging in a stable.

LECTURE 5.

INFANCY OF CHRIST.

Subdivisions:—The shepherds at night—The wise men from the east—Presentation in the temple—The flight into Egypt—The slaughter of the innocents. Ref. Matt. 2; Luke 2.

Self-review:—1. How did the shepherds learn of the Savior's birth? 2. How were the wise men apprised of His birth? 3. How did Herod's advisers determine His birthplace? 4. Where was Jesus taken and blessed when a child? 5. What murderous plan was adopted by Herod to slay the infant Savior? 6. How was the child's life preserved?

LECTURE 6.

CHILDHOOD OF CHRIST.

Subdivisions:—The passover at Jerusalem—Journey homeward—His discussion with the doctors in the temple—His inspirational reply to his mother—His respect for parental authority. Ref. Luke 2.

Self-review:—1. What national event called the parents of Jesus to Jerusalem annually? 2. Why were the doctors amazed at Him in the temple? 3. What answer did He make to His mother indicating that He apprehended the nature of His mission? 4. What glorious example of filial affection was set at this time? 5. What is said of His development? (Luke 2, 52.)

LECTURE 7.

CALLING OF JOHN THE BAPTIST.

Subdivisions:—His message to the people—His declaration concerning the Savior. Time, 26 A. D. Ref. Luke 3; John 1.

Self-review:—1. Who sent John on his mission? (Mark 1, 2; Luke 1, 17; John 1, 6.) 2. What was the special message John bore to the peple? 3. What declaration did he make concerning the Savior? 4. What was the cause of John's imprisonment? 5. At whose request was John beheaded?

LECTURE 8.

BAPTISM OF THE SAVIOR.

Subdivisions:—Place—Proper authority—The manner of His baptism—Why He was baptized—The testimony of the Holy Ghost. Time, 27 A. D. Ref. Matt. 3; Mark 1.

Self-review:—1. Where was Jesus baptized? 2. What was the necessity of His being baptized? 3. Show that he was baptized by immersion. 4. How did God the Father testify His pleasure at this act? 5. What sign of the Holy Ghost was given?

LECTURE 9.

THE TEMPTATION OF THE SAVIOR.

Subdivisions:—The nature of it—The object—His scriptural replies. Time, 27 A. D. Ref. Matt. 4; Luke 4.

Self-review:—1. Where did Jesus go immediately after His baptism? 2. How long did He stay in the wilderness? 3. What temptations by Satan are here mentioned? 4. What answers did the Savior make to the tempter? 5. How do His answers prove that He had been a careful student of the scriptures?

LECTURE 10.

CHRIST'S PROCLAMATION OF HIS AUTHORITY.

Subdivisions:—His customary attendance at Sabbath worship—The prophetic text—His announcement of its fulfillment—His expulsion from the synagogue—His escape from the mob. Time, 31 A. D. Ref. Luke 4.

Self-review:—1. Where did the parents of Jesus reside? 2. Show that He was a regular attendant at Sabbath service. 3. Find the verse in the Bible which Jesus read in proclaiming His authority. 4. How did the people receive His proclamation? 5. How did He escape from the mob?

LECTURE 11.
CALLING OF THE TWELVE APOSTLES.

Subdivisions:—The nature of the apostleship—Names of the Twelve Apostles. Time, 31 A. D. Ref. Matt. 3; Luke 6.

Self-review:— 1. What is meant by an Apostle of Jesus Christ? 2. Give the names of the Twelve Apostles chosen at Jerusalem. 3. Give the names of the Twelve Nephite Apostles chosen by the Savior. (3 Nephi, 19.) 4. Name the first twelve members of the quorum of Apostles in this dispensation. 5. Name the present members of the quorum of the Twelve.

LECTURE 12.
THE TRANSFIGURATION.

Subdivisions:—The three select apostles—The two Divine ministers—The admonition of secrecy given to the three apostles. Time, 32 A. D. Ref. Mark 9; Luke 9; Life of Joseph Smith, p. 498.

Self-review:—1. What is meant by transfiguration? 2. Name the three Apostles who witnessed the transfiguration. 3. Who were the two special heavenly ministers that conferred with Jesus on this occasion? 4. What special charge did Jesus give to the three Apostles just after the transfiguration? 5. What divine testimony was heard by the three Apostles during the transfiguration?

LECTURE 13.
THE APPOINTMENT OF THE SEVENTY.

Subdivisions:—The character of the appointment—The missionary instructions given to the Seventy. Time, 33 A. D. Ref. Luke 10.

Self-review:—1. What is the special calling of a Seventy? 2. Explain the organization of the Seventies. (Doc. and Cov. Sec. 107. 3. How were the Seventies sent out in the days of the Savior? 4. What special instructions were given to the Seventies? 5. Name the present first seven presidents of Seventies.

LECTURE 14.
· CHRIST'S ENTRY INTO JERUSALEM.

Subdivisions: — The prophetic preparation — The triumphal march — The assertion of His authority in the temple—The Pharisee mob —The Sadducees' presumptive interrogation —The Pharisaico-Sadducee conspiracy. Time, 33 A. D. Ref. Matt. 21; Luke 19.

Self-review:—1. How did Jesus enter Jerusalem on this

occasion? 2. What special demonstration was made by the people?
3. How did He manifest righteous indignation at the desecration
of the temple? 4. What did Jesus do day after day after He had
ejected the desecrators? 5. How did He silence the presumptuous
and hypocritical questioning of the Sadducees?

LECTURE 15.
THE LORD'S SUPPER.

Subdivisions:—The preparation—The sacredness of the ordinance instituted—The condemnation consequent upon its abuse.
Ref. Matt. 26; Mark 14; Luke 22; John, 12, 13.

Self-review:—1. Who instituted the sacrament of the Lord's
supper? (Luke xxii, 14-20.) 2. What special preparations
were made for this supper? 3. Who were the partakers of this
supper? 4. What is the special purpose of the Lord's supper?
5. What are the conditions of worthiness to partake of the supper
or sacrament? 6. What is the condemnation consequent upon
the abuse of the sacredness of this holy ordinance?

LECTURE 16.
CHRIST IN THE GARDEN OF GETHSEMANE.

Subdivisions:—The sorrowful watchers—The thrice repeated
prayer—The Savior's sublime recognition of, and perfect obedience
to His Father's will—The betrayal. Ref. Matt. 26; Mark 14;
Luke 22.

Self-review:—1. Where is the Garden of Gethsemane? 2. For
what purpose did Jesus and His apostles visit the garden? 3. What
spirit seemed to overpower the apostles at Gethsemane? 4. Repeat
the Savior's remarkable prayer on this trying occasion. 5. What
sublime lesson of perfect love is taught in this complete recognition of His Father's will? 6. How was the Savior delivered
unto the mobocratic priestcraft? 7. Why would He not allow
His apostles to defend Him?

LECTURE 17.
THE MOCK TRIAL AND CONDEMNATION.

Subdivisions:—Before the High Priests—Before Herod
—Before Pilate—The brutal scourging—On the way to Golgotha.
Ref. Matt. 26; Mark 14; Luke 22, 23; John 18.

Self-review:—1. Where was Jesus taken for the first mock
trial? 2. On what testimony did the high priest condemn Him

to die? 3. Before whom was He taken after His illegal condemnation by Caiaphas the high priest? 4. Why did Pilate, the Roman governor, send Jesus to Herod, the king? 5. What was the nature and result of the trial before Herod? 6. What was Pilate's testimony concerning the innocence of Jesus? 7. What lamentable defect in the government was plainly manifest in this instance where a citizen is left to the fury of a brutal mob after being twice found innocent by the highest civil authority?

LECTURE 18.
THE CRUCIFIXION AND BURIAL.

Subdivisions:—The manner of execution—The throes of nature on both continents—The time on the cross—The obtaining of the body by Joseph—The preparation of the body for the sepulchre—The time in the tomb. Ref. Matt. 27; Mark 15; Key to Theology.

Self-review: —1. What is the meaning of the word crucifixion? 2. How did nature manifest her grief at this awful crime? 3. What occurred in the temple during the agonies on the cross? 4. What took place on the western continent during the brutal mobocratic execution of the Savior? 5. How long was He on the cross? 6. Who obtained possession of, and prepared the body for burial? 7. Describe the sepulchre in which the body of Jesus lay. 8. What futile efforts were made by his infidel enemies to prevent His predicted resurrection? 9. How long was the body in the tomb?

LECTURE 19.
THE RESURRECTION OF OUR SAVIOR.

Subdivisions.—The Christian Sabbath dawn—The angel of life, awful to the guards, but comforting to the friends of Jesus—His refusal to be touched before ascending to His Father,—The bribing of the guards by the high priests. Ref. Matt. 28; Mark 16; Luke 24; John 20.

Self-review:—1. On which day of the week was the resurrection? 2. Who first saw Him after His resurrection? 3. Why did He refuse to be touched at that time? 4. What object did the chief priests have in bribing the Roman soldiers? 5. Where was Jesus while His body lay in the tomb?

LECTURE 20.
FROM THE RESURRECTION TO THE ASCENSION.

Subdivisions:—His appearance to Mary—His walk and talk

with two of His disciples unrecognized—His appearance to the eleven—His last will and testament. Time, 33 A. D. Ref. Matt. 28; Mark 16; Luke 24.

Self-review:—1. How did He make Himself known to the two disciples with whom He walked and talked unrecognized? 2. How did He make Himself known unto the eleven? 3. What did He say concerning the Gospel of repentance and remission of sins? 4. What reason did He give for directing His Apostles to tarry at Jerusalem for a time? 5. What was His last will and testament?

LECTURE 21.
THE ASCENSION.

Subdivisions:—Christ's sudden disappearance from the eleven disciples—The wonderment of the men of Galilee who witnessed the ascension—The testimony of the two heavenly messengers as to His return to the earth. Ref. Mark 16; Luke 24; Acts 1.

Self-review:—1. Describe the sudden disappearance of the Savior from His disciples. 2. Where did His ascension take place? 3. Who witnessed His ascension? 4. What was the testimony of the two heavenly messengers? 5. Whom did He declare should be His witnesses to all the world?

LECTURE 22.
THE DAY OF PENTECOST.

Subdivisions:—The mutual meeting of the Apostles—The calling of Matthias to the Apostleship in the Pentecostal feast—The gift of tongues—Peter's powerful discourse—The material and spiritual oneness. Ref. Acts 1, 2.

Self-review:—1. Explain the meaning of the word Pentecost. 2. What important business was transacted by the Apostles on the day of Pentecost? 3. What spiritual manifestation was made on that day? 4. How was the vacancy in the quorum of the Twelve filled? 5. What did the Apostle Peter tell the people to do to be saved?

LECTURE 23.
THE IMPRISONMENT OF THE APOSTLES.

Subdivisions:—The false charge—The mock trial—The incarceration—The deliverance—Gamaliel's defense of religious liberty. Time, 33 A. D. Ref. Acts 4, 5.

Self-review:—1. Why were the Apostles imprisoned? 2. What was Peter's testimony in regard to his authority? 3. How were the

Apostles delivered from prison? 4. What was Peter's reply when forbidden to preach the Gospel? 5. What professional man defended the Apostles during their persecution?

LECTURE 24.

THE MARTYR STEPHEN.

Subdivisions:—His deaconship—His miraculous works—His meekness—His brutal execution. Time, 33 A. D. Ref. Acts 6, 7.

Self-review:—1. What office did Stephen the martyr hold? 2. Name the six deacons specially called to assist Stephen. 3. What was the special work required of these deacons? 4. What was the charge preferred against Stephen? 5. What manner of death did he suffer?

LECTURE 25.

PAUL, THE APOSTLE TO THE GENTILES.

Subdivisions:—His conversion—His zealous advocacy of the Gospel—His miracles—His whipping, imprisonment, and deliverance—His occupation as a tent-maker—His rescue from the mob at Jerusalem—His Roman citizenship—His trial before the Jewish council—His hearing before Felix—His summons before Festus—His appeal to Cæsar—His defense before Agrippa—His journey to Rome—His teachings while in custody, in Rome, two years. Time, 35-62 A. D. Ref. Acts 9, 15, 16, 21, 22.

Self-review::—1. Rehearse Paul's conversion. 2. Why was he whipped and imprisoned? 3. How was he delivered from prison? 4. Who rescued him from the mob at Jerusalem? 5. For what was he tried before the Jewish council? 6. Why was he summoned before Festus? 7. Why did he appeal to Cæsar? 8. What was his defense? 9. What did he do while in custody in Rome?

CHURCH HISTORY.*

DISPENSATION OF THE FULLNESS OF TIMES.

SUBJECT 1.

JOSEPH THE PROPHET.

Subdivisions.—His ancestry and birth. (1805, Vt.)—His first vision. (N. Y. 1820.) (Book of Mormon. II Nephi, 3.)

Self-review.—1. Of what lineage was the Prophet Joseph? (Key to Theology, p. 83.)   2. Where and when was Joseph Smith born? 3. What prediction was made concerning Joseph before his birth by his paternal grandfather, Asael Smith?   4. What led to his first vision in 1820?   5. What was revealed to him by the heavenly messengers?   6   What was made known to him in answer to prayer on the evening of September 21, 1823?   7. What prophecy recorded in the Book of Mormon, uttered by Joseph who was sold into Egypt, was fulfilled in the calling of Joseph Smith? (II Nephi, 3.)

SUBJECT 2.

THE PLATES OF GOLD.

Subdivisions:—Revealing of the plates by the Angel Moroni (1823). (See Book of Mormon, Moroni, 10.) - Delivery of the plates to Joseph.   (1827.)

Self-review:—1. Describe the plates.   (Life of Joseph Smith, p. 366.   Answers to Questions, p. 38.   Historical Record, p. 63.)   2. Where, when, and by whom were the plates shown to Joseph?   3. From whom did Joseph receive special instructions annually preparing him for the sacred charge of receiving the plates of records? 4. What other sacred things were with the plates?   5. When and by whom were they delivered?   6. To whom did Joseph return the plates?   (Pearl of Great Price, p. 68.)

SUBJECT 3.

TRANSLATION OF THE PLATES.

Subdivisions:—The Urim and Thummim—Exhibition of the

---

* For reference see Life of Joseph Smith, by George Q. Cannon. Historical Record by Andrew Jenson. *Juvenile Instructor,* commencing with Vol. 2. *Millennial Star,* commencing with the supplement to Vol. 14, to Vol 25. *Contributor,* Compendium. Pearl of Great Price.

4

characters by Martin Harris to Prof. Anthon and Dr. Mitchell, of
New York. (See Is., 29.)—Oliver the scribe—Publication of the
Book of Mormon. (1827-30, N. Y.)

Self-review:—1. In what characters were the engravings on the
plates? 2. How were they translated? (Key to Theology. Answers to Questions.) 3. Give a short account of the Urim and
Thummim. (Doc. and Cov., Sec. 17. Life of Nephi, p. 31. Life
of Joseph, p. 49.) 4. What was the testimony of Prof. Anthon of
New York, concerning the characters? 5. What ancient prophecy
was this declaration by Prof. Anthon in fulfillment of? (Is. 29.)

Subject 4.
THE WITNESSES TO THE PLATES.

Subdivisions:—Testimony of the Three Witnesses—Testimony
of the Eight Witnesses. (N. Y., 1829. Book of Mormon, II
Nephi, 27.)

Self-review:—1. Name the Three Witnesses to the plates containing the Book of Mormon. 2. Make a careful copy of their
testimony. 3. Name the Eight Witnesses. 4. Make a careful,
neat copy of their testimony. 5. What ancient prophecy was fulfilled by the testimony of these witnesses? (II Nephi, 27.)

Subject 5.
RESTORATION OF THE HOLY PRIESTHOOD.

Subdivisions:—The Aaronic or Levitical Priesthood; by John
the Baptist. (Harmony, Penn., May 15th, 1829.)—The higher or
Melchisedek Priesthood, by the Apostles Peter, James and John
(1829.)

Self-review:—1. What is meant by the Aaronic or Levitical
Priesthood? 2. Where, when, and by whom was the Priesthood
of Aaron restored? 3. Upon whom was this priesthood conferred?
4. Repeat the words of John the Baptist in restoring the Aaronic
Priesthood. 5. What is meant by the Melchisedek Priesthood? 6.
Why is it called the Melchisedek Priesthood? 7. Where, when,
by whom, and upon whom was this Higher Priesthood conferred?
(*Contributor*, Vol. X., pp. 307-311. Life of Joseph, p. 73.)

Subject 6.
ORGANIZATION OF THE CHURCH OF JESUS CHRIST OF LATTER-DAY SAINTS.

(Fayette, Seneca Co., New York, U. S. A., April 6, 1830.)
Self-review:—1. Name place and time in full of the organization

of the Church. 2. Give the names of the first six members. 3. How was the time and manner of organization determined? 4. Why was the Church called after the name of Jesus Christ? (Catechism, p. 52.) 5. By whom was it accepted? (Life of Joseph Smith, p. 75.)

SUBJECT 7.

ORDINANCES OF THE GOSPEL.

Subdivisions:—Baptisms—Confirmations—Ordinations — Institution of the Lord's Supper. (Book of Mormon, III Nephi 26. Mark 14; Luke 22; John 12, 13.)

Self-review:—1. Relate the conditions connected with the ordinances of baptism and confirmation. (See Pearl of Great Price, pp. 73-74.) 2. Mention the ordinances of the Gospel that were officiated in at the time of the organization of the Church. (Comp. p. 306.) 3. What is meant by the Lord's Supper? 4. By what other terms is the Lord's Supper known? 5. Show that the institution of the Lord's Supper was established in the Nephite Church; also in the Church at Jerusalem. (III Nephi 26. Mark 14; Luke 22; John 12, 13.)

SUBJECT 8.

PROCLAMATION OF THE GOSPEL AND FIRST GENERAL CHURCH CONFERENCE. (1830)

Self-review:—1. Where was the first public discourse in this dispensation, on the principles of the Gospel as revealed to Joseph, preached? 2. Where and when was the first conference of the Church held? (Life of Joseph, p. 85. Historical Record, p. 375.) 3. What was the result of the great faith of the congregation on this occasion? (Life of Joseph, p. 86.) 4. Where is Fayette? 5. When were the first missionaries appointed to the Lamanites? (Ibid p. 99.)

SUBJECT 9.

CALLING OF SPECIAL CHURCH OFFICERS.

Subdivisions:—First Bishop—First Church Historian and Recorder—Ordaining High Priests. (1831.)

Self-review:—1: Who was the first presiding Bishop of the Church? 2. Who constitute the present presiding Bishopric? 3. Who was the first Church Historian and Recorder? 4. Who is the present Historian and Church Recorder? 5. Show the sacredness of the office of Recorder.

Subject 10.

GATHERING AND TEMPLE BUILDING.

(Kirtland, Ohio, 1831-36.)

Self-review.--1. Where was the first gathering place of the Saints? (Life of Joseph Smith, p. 104. Hist. Rec., p. 391.) 2. When was the land of Zion dedicated for the gathering place of the Saints? (Comp. p. 306.) 3. What early provision was made for the care of the poor and needy? (Life of Joseph Smith, pp. 108-9.) 4. Where was the first temple built in this dispensation? 5. Name, give location, and date of building of the temples in this dispensation.

Subject 11.

LAND OF ZION.

Subdivisions:—Dedication of the land – Choosing of the temple site. (Mo., 1831.)

Self-review:—1. What is Zion? 2. Where is the land of Zion? 3. Where is the center place of the land of Zion? (Life of Joseph Smith, p. 118.) 4. Where, when, and by whom was the spot for the temple site in the land of Zion dedicated? (Life of Joseph Smith, pp. 118-19.) 5. Write alphabetically the names of all the Stakes of Zion to date. 6. What and where is Adam-ondi-Ahman? (Hist. Rec., p. 45.)

Subject 12.

COMPILATION AND PUBLICATION OF THE REVELATIONS AND COMMANDMENTS, OR DOCTRINE AND COVENANTS. (1832.)

Self-review:—1. By what name is the Book containing the Revelations and Commandments known? 2. When and by whom were the "Commandments" arranged for publication? (Life of Joseph Smith, p. 126.) 3. When was the Book of Doctrine and Covenants first published? (Life of Joseph Smith, p. 133.) 4. Where and at what gathering was this publication ordered? (Ibid, p. 133.) 5. What does this book contain?

Subject 13.

CHURCH ORGANIZATIONS.

Subdivisions:—First Presidency of Three—Standing High Council. (Kirtland, Ohio, 1833-34.)

Self-review:—1. What constitutes the First Presidency of the Church? 2. Give the names of the first quorum of three who presided over the Church in this dispensation? 3. Who are the

members of the First Presidency of the Church to-day? 4. What
is the standing High Council? (Doc. and Cov.) 5. Where
and when was the first standing High Council organized? (Doc.
and Cov., Sec. 102. Hist. Rec., p. 413.) 6. How many High
Councils are there?

SUBJECT 14.
ORGANIZATIONS, Continued.

Subdivisions:—Quorum of the Twelve Apostles. (See also
Mark 3; Luke 6. III Nephi, 11, 12, 18.)—First Quorum of Seventies. (See also Luke 10.) (Kirtland, 1835.)

Self-review:—1. What is an apostle? (Doc. and Cov.) 2.
Where and when was the first quorum of the Twelve Apostles
called? 3. From what body of men were members of the first
quorum of the Twelve Apostles, and the first quorum of the
Seventies selected? (Life of Joseph Smith, pp. 182-86.) 4. Name
the members of the first quorum of Twelve Apostles in this dispensation. 5. Name the present members of the Twelve Apostles.

SUBJECT 15.
DEDICATION OF THE KIRTLAND TEMPLE.

Visit of the Savior, Moses, Elias, and Elijah. (1836)

Self-review:—1. Where is Kirtland? 2. Where and when was
the first temple in this dispensation built? 3. What glorious
manifestations occurred at the dedication of the Kirtland Temple?
(Life of Joseph Smith, pp. 193-8.) 4. Who were the heavenly
messengers at this dedication? (Doc. and Cov., Sec. 110.) 5. What
special keys and powers were restored at this time?

SUBJECT 16.
OPENING OF FOREIGN MISSIONS.
(1836-37.)

Self-review:—1. To which foreign nation was the Gospel first
sent? 2. Who was called to preside over this mission? 3. Where
and when was the first baptism in England performed? 4. Who
was reigning in England at the time the Gospel was first introduced
into that land? 5. What favorable omen greeted the eyes of the
missionaries upon their landing? (Life of Joseph Smith, p. 214.)

SUBJECT 17.
GATHERING IN MISSOURI.

Temple site at Far West located—Law of Tithing revealed. (1837-8.)

Self-review:—1. Where is Far West? (Hist. Rec., pp. 719-20.)

2. When was the site for a temple at Far West located?   (Hist.
Rec., p. 721.)   3. What events have transpired to render Far West
forever memorable?   4. Relate the circumstances of the renewel of
the ancient tithe covenant.   (Life of Joseph Smith, pp. 180-81.) 5.
When was the law of Tithing revealed?   (Doc. and Cov.)

SUBJECT 18.

FOUNDING NAUVOO AND BUILDING THE TEMPLE THERE.

(1839-46.)

Self-review:—1. What is the meaning of the word Nauvoo?   2.
Describe the location of Nauvoo, The Beautiful.   (Hist. Rec., p. 744.)
3. What was the sanitary condition of the locality at the time the
beloved prophet and his people began settlement there?   (Life of
Joseph Smith, pp. 291-94.)   4. When and by whom was Nauvoo
founded?   5. Describe the ceremony of laying the corner stones of
the Nauvoo temple.   (Life of Joseph Smith, pp. 345-47.) 6. When
was the Nauvoo temple dedicated?   (Hist. Rec., Vol. IX, p. 27.)

SUBJECT 19.

THE WORK ABROAD.

(1839-40.)

Self-review:—1. Prepare a list of the nations in chronological
order which have permitted the introduction of the Gospel.   (Answers to Questions, pp. 30-37.)   2. Point out on your map the
countries into which the Gospel has been introduced.   3. Mention
the political powers that have forbidden the preaching of the Gospel.
(Answers to Questions, pp., 30-37.)   4. What is the oldest continuous Church periodical now published?   6. What ancient revelation
is being brought to pass by this divinely authorized missionary
work?   (Rev. 14.)

SUBJECT 20.

ORGANIZATION OF THE RELIEF SOCIETY.

(Nauvoo, Ill., March 17, 1842.)

Self-review:—1. What is the design of the Relief Society? (Hist.
Rec., p. 490.)   2. Where, when, and by whom was the society organized?   3. Who was the first president?   4. What revelation
was the election of Emma Smith as president in fulfillment of? (Doc.
and Cov., Sec. 25.)   5. Who is the present president?

SUBJECT 21.

ASSASSINATION OF JOSEPH THE PROPHET AND HYRUM THE PATRIARCH.

(Carthage, Hancock Co., Ills., June 27, 1844.)

Self-review:—1. How were the Prophet and Patriarch betrayed finally into the hands of their murderers? (Hist. Rec., pp., 558-9.) 2. Where and when were Joseph and Hyrum assassinated? 3. Under whose official protection were they at the time? 4. Who remained with them in jail during this horrible tragedy? 5. Relate the circumstances of the assassination in brief as recorded in the Book of Doctrine and Covenants.

SUBJECT 22.

PERSECUTIONS, MOBBINGS AND DRIVINGS.

(New York and Ohio.)

Self-review:—1. To what violence was Joseph subjected on his return from Cumorah with the plates? (Life of Joseph Smith, pp., 50-51. "Remarkable Visions by O. Pratt.) 2. What treatment did he receive from the religious preachers of the day? 3. What attempts were made to rob him of the plates on his way from Manchester, N. Y., to Harmony, Penn.? (Hist. Rec., p. 364.) 4. What was the result of the arrests and trial at Colesville, N. Y.? Life of Joseph Smith, pp. 87-90.) 5. Describe the "Night of Fury" at Hiram, O., March 25, 1832. (Life of Joseph Smith, pp. 128-31.)

SUBJECT 23.

PERSECUTIONS, MOBBINGS AND DRIVINGS, Continued.

(Ohio and Mo.)

Self-review:—1. Relate briefly the mobbing at Independence, the Center Stake, in the summer of 1833. (Life of Joseph Smith, pp. 146-152. 2. What can you say of Lieut-Governor Boggs' organized militia-mob of Nov. 5, 1833? (Ibid, p. 162.) 3. What divine interposition saved Joseph and Zion's Camp from the organized mob on Fishing River? (Ibid, pp. 168-72.) 4. Describe the pursuit of the Prophet and his counselors by the infuriated mob for more than two hundred miles from Kirtland to Far West. (Ibid, p. 223.) 5. How did Joseph and Sydney escape assassination on their way from Buffalo to Kirtland in Aug., 1837? (Ibid, pp. 217-18.)

Subject 24.

PERSECUTIONS, MOBBINGS AND DRIVINGS, Continued.

(Missouri to Illinois.)

Self-review:—1. When did the appalling mob crusade begin which resulted finally in the exile of the Saints from the State of Missouri? (Life of Joseph Smith, p. 230.) 2. What noble defense of the most sacred right of American citizenship was made at the polls at Gallatin, Mo., in 1838? (Ibid, pp. 231-32.) 3. Show that hireling politicians and preachers, pretending to be followers of the Savior, were leaders of mobs who robbed, plundered, murdered and drove loyal American citizens from their homes in De Witt, Mo., in 1838. (Ibid, pp. 244-48. Hist. Rec., p. 603.) 4. Describe the massacre at Haun's Mill. (Ibid, pp. 252-255.) 5. What were the character and result of General Lucas' Mobocratic Preachers' "Court Martial" of Nov. 1, 1838? (Ibid, pp. 256-264.) 6. What was the result of the final appeal for redress of the highest authority of the land? (Ibid, pp. 303-306.)

Subject 25.

EXODUS FROM ILLINOIS, U. S. A., TO MEXICAN TERRITORY.

(1846-47.)

Self-review:—1. When were the Saints driven from their homes in Illinois? 2. In what country did they find a home and plant the flag of liberty? 3. Show on a large map before the association the route taken by the pioneers from the Mississippi to Great Salt Lake. 4. Show the route taken by the Mormon Battalion from Winter Quarters to Salt Lake Valley, *via* Santa Fe and San Diego. (Hist. Mormon Battalion, pp. 364-68.) 5. Read extracts from Historical Address of Gen. Thomas L. Kane, describing the "expulsion of the Saints from Nauvoo." (Hist. Rec., p. 839. Answers to Questions, by Geo. A. Smith, pp. 13-15. Hand-book of Reference, pp. 19-24.)

ENGLISH HISTORY.*

BRITAIN.

READING I.
ANCIENT ENGLAND AND THE ROMANS.

Time, B. C. 50 to A. D. 450—500 years. Ref. ch. 1.

Self-review:—1. What is the origin of the word England? 2. Give the location of England. 3. Who were the Phœnicians? 4. What was the ancient religion of the Britains? 5. When did Julius Cæsar conquer England?

THE SAXONS.
Time, 450 to 1016.
READING 2.

Ancient England under the early Saxons (450 to 871—421 yrs.); and the reign of Alfred the Great (871 to 901—30 yrs.), and Edward the Elder (901 to 925—24 years.) Ref. chs. 2, 3.

Self-review:—1. Who were the Saxons? 2. In what regard were the Saxons like the North American Indians? 3. By whom was Christianity introduced into England? 4. Who was Alfred the Great? 5. Under whose reign were the seven petty kingdoms of England united?

READING 3.

England under Athelstane (925 to 941—16 yrs.) and the Reign of the Six Boy-Kings (941 to 1016—75 yrs) Ref. ch. 4.

Self-review:—1. Mention three important things accomplished by Athelstane. 2. Who was the first of the six boy-kings? 3. What is said of the priests in the days of the six boy-kings? 4. Name the remaining five boy-kings. 5. Why was Ethelred, the last of the boy-kings, nick-named "The Unready?"

THE DANES AND RESTORED SAXONS.
Time, 1016 to 1066.
READING 4.

England under Canute the Dane (1016 to 1035), and Harold Harefoot, Hardicanute, and Edward the Confessor (1035 to 1066.)

*These readings are pursued from Dickens' History of England, M. I. Series.

England under Harold the Second and conquered by the Normans in the same year.   Ref chs. 5, 6, 7.

Self-review:—1. What great lesson is taught by the anecdote of Canute commanding the sea?   2. What seemed to have been the principal delight of the kings in these days?   3. What is a monk? 4. What king pretended to heal people by touching them?   5. What is meant by Peter's Pence?   6. Write a short story of the battle of Hastings.   (pp. 73-78.)

THE NORMANS.

Time, 1066 to 1154.

READING 5.

England under William the First, called the Conqueror (1066 to 1087—21 years), and the Reign of William the Second, called Rufus (1087 to 1100—13 years)   Ref. chs. 8, 9.

Self-review:—1. Narrate the circumstance of the crowning of William the Conqueror in Westminster Abbey.   2. What is the origin of the Curfew?   3. Who was Peter the Hermit?   4. What were the crusades?   5. How and by whom was the "New Forest" made?

READING 6.

England under Henry the First, called Fine-Scholar (1100 to 1135—35 yrs.), and reign of Matilda and Stephen (1135 to 1154— 19 yrs.)   Ref. chs. 10, 11.

Self-review:—1. By what declarations did Henry the First begin his reign?   2. Tell the story of the "White Ship."   3. Why did Henry the First have the poet's eyes put out?   4. What became of all of King Henry's plans?   5. What can you say of King Stephen's reign altogether?

THE PLANTAGENETS.

Time, 1154 to 1485—331 years.

READING 7.

England under Henry the Second (1154 to 1189—35 years.) and Reign of Richard the First, called Lion Heart (1189 to 1199— 10 yrs.)   Ref. chs. 12, 13.

Self-review:—1. Name some of the important acts beginning Henry Plantagenet's reign.   2. Tell the story of Thomas à Becket. 3. Describe the pageantry of the new Archbishop of Canterbury. 4. How did Richard the First raise means to fit out an army to go on a crusade to the Holy Land?   5. What king joined him in the crusade?

Reading 8.

England under John, called Lackland (1199 to 1216 –17 yrs.), and Reign of Henry the Third (1216 to 1272—56 yrs). Ref. chs. 14, 15. .

Self-review: – 1. Why was Prince Arthur so much hated by King John? 2. What is the Magna Charta? 3. What was the fate of King John? 4. Name some improvements made by Lord Pembroke, the Regent. 5. What followed the decision of the King of France between the King and Barons of England respecting the Great Charter and the "Committee of Government?"

Reading 9.

England under Edward the First (1272 to 1307—35 yrs.), and Reign of Edward the Second (1307 to 1327—20 yrs.) Ref chs. 16, 17.

Self-review:—1. Describe the coronation feast at the crowning of Edward the First and his Queen. 2. How were the Jews treated during the reign of Edward the First? 3. What was the result of the effort of Edward the First to unite England, Scotland, and Wales under one sovereign? 4. Who was the first Prince of Wales? 5. What can you say of the great battle of Bannockburn?

Reading 10.

Reign of Edward the Third. (1327 to 1377—50 yrs) Ref. ch. 18.

Self-review:—1. Relate the circumstances of the capture and death of Roger Mortimer. 2. What was the first important effort of King Edward the Third? 3. Who was the Black Prince? 4. What can you say of the treaty of the "Great Peace?" 5. Mention five things for which the reign of Edward the Third was memorable.

Reading 11.

Reign of Richard the Second. (1377 to 1399—22 yrs.) Ref. ch. 19.

Self-review: – 1. How was Richard the Second regarded by the whole English nation? 2. What is the origin of the English Polltax? 3. Describe the Poll-tax uprising. 4. What were the conditions proposed by the rioters to the King? 5. Relate the circumstances of the deposing of King Richard the Second and the seating on the throne of his cousin Henry.

Reading 12.

Reign of Henry the Fourth, called Bolingbroke. (1399 to 1413 --14 yrs.) Ref. ch. 20.

Self-review:—1. Who were the Lollards?   2. What infamous tribunal for the punishment of persons for their opinions, was established by Henry the Fifth?   3. What was the fate of King Richard? 4. What is said of the superstitions of the times?   5. How was young James the heir to the Scottish throne treated?

READING 13.

England under Henry the Fifth. (1413 to 1422—9 yrs.) Ref. ch. 21.

Self-review:—1. Mention four important things done by King Henry the Fifth in the beginning of his reign.   2. Why was the battle of Agincourt so called?   3. What can you say of what was known as the "Perpetual Peace?"   4. What demand was made by King Henry upon the King of France?   5. What followed the refusal of the French to accede to his demand?   6. What were the conditions of peace between England and France?   7. Describe the funeral of King Henry the Fifth.

READING 14.

Reign of Henry the Sixth. (1422 to 1461—39 yrs.) Ref. ch. 22.

Self-review:—1. Whom did Henry the Sixth succeed?   2. What was the result of crowning Charles the Seventh?   3. Who was Joan of Arc?   4. What did the Maid of Orleans do?   5. What was the origin of the War of the Roses?   6. Why was it called the War of the Roses?

READING 15.

England under Edward the Fourth. (1461 to 1483—22 yrs.), and Reign of Edward the Fifth for a few weeks. Ref. chs. 23, 24.

Self-review:—1. Describe the first great battle of the War of the Roses.   2. Why was the Earl of Warwick called the king-maker? 3. Explain the titles Duke, Duchess, Earl and Lord as used in history.   4. What condition of society was illustrated by the treatment of Jane Shore?   5. As a student of history, what is your opinion in regard to the following: "Education is the cheapest defense of the nation?"

READING 16.

Reign of Richard the Third. (1483 to 1485—2 yrs.) Ref. ch. 25.

Self-review:—1. How many times was Richard the Third crowned?   2. How did he dispose of his two nephews?   3. What became of his wife, the queen?   4. Why did he not marry the Princess Elizabeth as he intended?   5. What state of mind fol-

lowed his crimes? 6. Describe the death of the villainous despot.
7. Who succeeded this usurper?

THE TUDORS.

Time 1485—1603—118 yrs.

READING 17.

England under Henry the Seventh (1485 to 1509—24 yrs.), and
Reign of Henry the Eighth (1509 to 1547—38 yrs.) Ref. chs. 26, 27.

Self-review:—1. What is meant by "Henry the Seventh?" 2.
Where were princes put for safe keeping in those days? 3. What
disease followed the public feasts? 4. What was the result of the
battle of Flodden Field? 5. In whose reign was the papal power
in England destroyed?

READING 18.

Reign of Henry the Eighth, concluded. (1533 to 1547—14 yrs.)
Ref. ch. 28.

Self-review:—1. How was the news of the marriage of Henry the
Eighth and Anne Boleyn received by the Pope, monks and friars?
2. Define the terms pope, monk, friar, cardinal, marquis, and
monasteries? 3. What is said of the suppression of many of the
English abbeys and monasteries? 4. Who was at the head of the
body of commissioners who began this work of vandalism? 5.
What is meant by "the whip with six strings?" 6. What important work was achieved during the reign of Henry the Eighth?

READING 19.

Reign of Edward the Sixth (1547 to 1553—6 yrs.) Ref. ch. 29.

Self-review:—1. What provisions were made for the government
of the kingdom while King Edward the Sixth was under age? 2.
What interpretation was given to the "curious" parts of the late
king's will? 3. What was the action of the new Duke of Somerset?
4. Of what religious belief was King Edward the Sixth? 5. Mention
one good and two bad acts of Parliament after Somerset's return
from invading Scotland. 6. Who were the most powerful of the
clergy during this reign? 7. Where was Somerset, the protector,
finally beheaded?

READING 20.

England under Mary (1553 to 1558—5 yrs.), and the reign of
Elizabeth (1558 to 1603—45 yrs.) Ref. chs. 30, 31.

Self-review:—1. What was the career of Lady Jane Grey? 2.
Who was Mary Queen of Scots? 3. How did Mary commence

her reign?   4. What was the fate of Bishops Latimer, Ridley and
Cranmer?   5. What is meant by the "Massacre of St. Bar-
tholomew?"   6. What was the "Spanish Armada?"   7. Mention
several things that make the reign of Elizabeth forever memorable?

THE STUARTS.

Time, 1603 to 1649 - 46 yrs.

READING 21.

Reign of James the First (1603 to 1625—22 yrs.)   Ref. ch. 32.
Self-review:—1. What was the cause of the disagreement between King James and his people?   2. What was his idea respecting government?   3. Explain the "Gunpowder Plot."   4. How
long was Sir Walter Raleigh confined in the Tower, and what did
he write while in prison?   5. What part did Raleigh take in
American history?

READING 22.

Reign of Charles the First. (1635 to 1649 – 34 years.) Ref. ch. 33.
Self-review:—1. Why was Queen Henrietta disliked by the
English people?   2. Why did this tyrant, Charles the First, dissolve
parliament?   3. How did he raise money?   4. What unconsti-
tutional decision was rendered in his favor?   5. What great revolution followed the oppressive administration of Charles the First?

THE COMMONWEALTH.

Time, 1649 to 1660—11 yrs.

READING 23.

The Council of State and Government by Parliament (1649 to
1653—4 yrs.);   The Protectorate of Oliver Cromwell (1653 to 1658
—5 yrs.);   The Protectorate of Richard Cromwell (seven months):
The Council of State and Government by Parliament (thirteen
months.)   Ref. ch. 34.

Self-review:—1. What act was passed by the House of Commons
on the memorable day of the execution of Charles the First?   2.
What was the Council of State appointed by the House of Com-
mons?   3. Who was made commander of all the forces of the
Commonwealth of England?   4. Relate the escape of Charles the
Second after the battle of Worcester.   5. Who succeeded Oliver
Cromwell?   6. Describe the change from Commonwealth to King.

READING 24.

Time, 1660 to 1688—28 yrs.

The reign of Charles the Second (1660 to 1685—25 yrs.), and

the reign of James the Second (1685 to 1688—3 yrs.) Ref. chs. 35, 36.

Self-review:—1. Of what kind of persons was the court of Charles the Second composed? 2. Mention some of his brutal executions of men who dared to oppose his tyranny. 3. What object did the clergy have in view when favoring the despotic King Charles the Second? 4. What was the Conventicle Act? 5. Describe the Great Plague of 1665. 6. Explain the Five-mile Act passed by Parliament just after the plague? 7. Describe the Great Fire of 1666. 8 What did Charles the Second do with the Parliament? 9. What is said of the Oxford University during the reign of Charles the Second? 10. What was the first act of James the Second? 11. What was the one chief object of his reign? 12. Who was the noted Jeffreys? 13. Why did James the Second favor Catholics? 14. State the chief distinction between Protestantism and Roman Catholicism.

THE REVOLUTION.

Time, 1688.

READING 25.

End of the Stuart Line; Re-establishment of the Protestant Church; Historical Thread:

Reign of William the Third (1689 to 1702—13 yrs.); Reign of Anne (1702 to 1713—11 yrs.; England under the Four Georges (1714 to 1830—116 yrs.); Reign of William the Fourth (1830 to 1837—7 yrs.); and reign of Queen Victoria (1837.) Ref. ch. 37.

Self-review:—1. What can you say of William the Third, Prince of Orange?· 2. In whose reign were England and Scotland incorporated under the name of Great Britain? 3. What four monarchs succeeded Queen Anne? 4. What rebellion occurred during the reign of George the Second? 5. What great country did England lose during the reign of George the Third? 6. What did that country become? 7. What is here said of the United States as a nation? 8. When did the union between Great Britain and Ireland take place? 9. Who succeeded George the Fourth? 10. Who is the present queen of England? 11. Give a short account of Victoria, the Mother Queen.

BIOGRAPHY.*

STUDY 1.

Subdivisions:—Nephi's personal character and education—Lehi and family at Jerusalem—The warning—The persecution—The commandment—The departure—The camp—The altar. Ref. chs. 1, 2.

Self-review:—1. Describe Jerusalem, the home of Lehi. 2. Of what lineage was Lehi? 3. What is said of Nephi's influence over his associates? 4. What is said of Nephi's influence in shaping the methods of government, forms of worship, and mode of life of the Nephite nation? 5. Why did Lehi and family leave Jerusalem?

STUDY 2.

Subdivisions:—Living faith—Revelation—Promised Land—Nephi's future—The return to Jerusalem—The plates. Ref. ch. 3.

Self-review:—1. How did Nephi obtain constant revelation for his guidance? 2. What is the Promised Land referred to? 3. What was to be Nephi's relation to his people in that land? 4. What was the object of the return to Jerusalem? 5. Why did they so much desire the records belonging to their father's house?

STUDY 3.

Subdivisions:—Laban and the records—Lehi's riches—The angel—The sword of Laban—The plates secured—Zoram. Ref. chs. 4, 5.

Self-review: —1. Who was Laban? 2. Which did Nephi consider of the greater value, the riches of his father or the records of his father's house? 3. What revelation to Nephi was confirmed by the angel of deliverance? 4. What was the final result of Nephi's efforts for the plates? 5. What was the Mosaic law respecting bondmen? 6. Who besides Nephi in this dispensation have seen the famous sword of Laban?

STUDY 4.

Subdivisions:—Successful return with the records into the

---

*The following fifteen studies are pursued from the "Life of Nephi," M. I. Series, by Prest. Geo. Q. Cannon. The ten "Selections from Irving," M. I. Series, make up twenty-five exercises for the year.

wilderness—Testimony of Sariah—Contents of the Plates—Their value—Second journey to Jerusalem—Ishmael and family—Nephi's persecution and miraculous deliverance from his brothers. Ref. ch. 6.

Self-review:—1. What was the testimony of Nephi's mother? 2. How did they celebrate the return of their sons? 3. What did the records on the plates contain? 4. Show that the obtaining of these plates became of incalculable benefit in maintaining and spreading the true civilization of the Nephite nation. 5. What is said of the spirit which prompts fighting against the truth?

STUDY 5.

Subdivisions:—Divine manifestation to Lehi—Seed and grain-gathering—Marriages—Necessary experience—Commandment to again travel—The Director or Liahona—Direction taken. Ref. ch. 7.

Self-review:—1. What was the effect of Lehi's dream or vision while in the Valley of Lemuel? 2. What five marriages took place there? 3. Contrast the training in the wilderness of the Nephites with that of the ancient Israelites. 4. How was the party guided? 5. What was the Director or Liahona? 6. Contrast the means employed to guide the Nephites with that guiding the Israelites. 7. How did the Liahona operate?

STUDY 6

Subdivisions:—Travel in the desert—Food—Misfortune—Writting on the Ball—Death—Rebellion—Conspiracy—Laman and Lemuel continue to doubt predictions concerning Jerusalem—Their confidence in the glorious city—Its capture—Laman and Lemuel's repentance. Ref. chs. 8, 9.

Self-review:—1. What remarkable coincidence of travel is mentioned in this lesson? 2. What animals were found along the line of this route? 3. Of what did the food of the party consist? 4. What misfortune befell the party? 5. How did Nephi learn where to find game? 6. Which one of their party was buried at Nahom? 7. What conspiracy followed? 8. What was the popular idea in Jerusalem at this time regarding prophets? 9. How did the Jews look upon Jerusalem? 10. When and by whom was Jerusalem captured?

STUDY 7.

Subdivisions:—Direction of travel—Time in the wilderness—Health of the party—"Araby the Blest"—Manner of traveling—

Habits acquired in the desert—Contrast between the two brothers.
Ref. chs. 10, 11.

Self-review:—1. In what direction did they travel? 2. How
long were they in the wilderness. 3. How do you account for the
excellent health of the entire party? 4. Describe Bountiful, or the
land adjoining it. 5. How did the party most probably travel?
6. What is said of the habits acquired in the wilderness? 7. Show
that the influence of Laman was potent for evil as Nephi's was for
good.

Study 8.

Subdivisions:—Nephi as leader—Ship-building—Faithlessness
—Divine instructions—Completion of the ship—Nephi's acknow-
ledged ability. Ref. ch. 12.

/   *Self-review:*—1. Who was practically the leader of the colony
from this time on? 2. Repeat the word of the Lord to Nephi regarding building the ship. 3. How did they obtain tools to work
with. 4. Contrast the doubt and perfidy of Nephi's brethren with
his own faith and integrity. 5. What is said of mountains as
places of worship?

Study 9.

Subdivisions:—The embarkation—Jacob and Joseph—The mutiny—The tempest—Nephi's heroism, fidelity and integrity—Completion of ocean voyage. Ref. ch. 13.

Self-review:—1. After the ship was completed what was the
word of command? 2 After fair sailing for some time what took
place among the passengers? 3. What followed the mutiny? 4.
What was the conduct of Nephi during the sad hour of confusion
and cruelty? 5. To what land did they finally arrive?

Study 10.

Subdivisions:—The landing—Farming begun at once—Animals found—Ores—The horse—The potato—Land of Liberty—
Promises—Prophecies—Hatred. Ref. chs. 14, 15.

Self-review:—1. Where did the company land? 2. What animals were found? 3. What ores were discovered? 4. What
vegetables were found? 5. Explain why this continent was so long
hidden from the world.

Study 11.

Subdivisions:—Nephi's efforts to save his brethren—The separation—Nephi's careful preservation of the Records, the Liahona, the Sword of Laban—The two sets of plates—Mormon's

Abridgment—Wisdom of God greater than cunning of the devil. Ref. ch. 16.

Self-review:—1. Show that Nephi did all in his power to save his brethren. 2. What was he now commanded to do? 3. What did he specially preserve and carry with him? 4. What was the purpose of the two sets of plates? 5. From which set was Mormon's abridgment made? 6. Show the wisdom of God over the deep cunning of the devil.

Study 12.

Subdivisions:—The northward journey—Land of Nephi—Land of Zarahemla—Land of Mormon—Extent of the Land of Nephi—Bolivia and Peru—South America called Lehi—North America called Mulek.

Self-review:—1. In what direction did the Nephites travel after the separation? 2. Where was the Land of Nephi, their permanent home? 3. Where was the Land of Zarahemla? 4. What is said of the Land of Mormon? 5. What was the probable extent of the Land of Nephi? 6. What was the whole of what is now known as South America called by the Nephites? 7. What was North America called? (Helaman, vi, 10.)

Study 13.

Subdivisions:—Descriptions of lands once occupied by Nephites—Agreement of ancient and modern accounts—Accounting for rapid recovery from effects of commotions and war—Health—Longevity. Ref. ch. 18.

Self-review:—1. Describe the land once occupied by the Nephites. 2. How do the productions of the land now agree with description of same in the Book of Mormon? 3. How is the rapid recovery from the effects of disasters, commotions and wars accounted for? 4. What is said of the healthfulness of the climate of the Land of Nephi? 5. What is said of the longevity of the people?

Study 14.

Subdivisions:—The two distinct nations—The Land of Nephi an earthly paradise—Nephi, the prophet, statesman, and mighty leader—His sublime, extensive, and accurate predictions—Literal fulfillment attested by the Latter-day Saints. Ref. ch. 19.

Self-review:—1. What two great nations grew up upon this continent? 2. What was the nature of the land to which Nephi and his company were led after the separation? 3. How long did

the Nephite nationality exist? 4. Show the greatness of Nephi as
a faithful servant of God. 5. Mention some of the remarkable
events that Nephi foresaw. 6. Who are witnesses to the literal
fulfillment of his predictions?

STUDY 15.

Subdivisions:—The small plates—A king anointed—Patriarchal
form of government—Jacob presides over the church—Probable
change of dynasty—Return to King Mosiah's union of Priestly and
Kingly authority—Nephi, a born leader—Successful as a mechanic,
miner, seaman, chemist, metallurgist, stock raiser, agriculturist,
manufacturer, and statesman—His expanded views of the rights
and equality of man—Liberty. Ref. chs. 20, 21.

Self-review:—1. What commandment was given concerning the
small plates? 2. Why did Nephi not become king? 3. How were
the successive kings designated? 4. What was the form of
government at that time? 5. Who presided over the church at
that time? 6. What is said of a subsequent change of dynasty and
Mosiah's union of priestly and kingly authority? 7. Write a short
essay on the career of Nephi.

SCIENCE.

FIRST BOOK OF NATURE.*

LECTURE 1.

THE KINGDOMS OF NATURE.

Subdivisions:—1. Animals; 2. Plants; 3. Minerals. Animals and plants belong to the class of living things; Minerals are dead. Ref. ch. 1.

Self-review:—1. What distinguishes *natural* from *artificial* things? 2. What are the essential differences between *living* and *dead* things? 3. What are animals? 4. What are plants? 5. What are minerals?

LECTURE 2.

KINDS OF ANIMALS.

Subdivisions:—1. Vertebrates, or animals possessing bones and red blood. Warm-blooded vertebrates include mammals and birds; cold-blooded vertebrates include reptiles, amphibians, and fishes. 2. Invertebrates or animals possessing no internal skeleton and no red blood, as insects, worms, mollusks and radiates. Ref. ch. 2.

Self-review:—1. What are the main subdivisions of the animal kingdom? 2. Give the essential differences between vertebrates and invertebrates. 3. Show, with illustrations, the difference between warm-blooded and cold-blooded animals. 4. What is meant by the bony skeleton of an animal? 5. State, with explanations, to which division of the animal kingdom each of the following belongs:— pigeon, squirrel, dog, frog, lizard.

LECTURE 3.

APES AND MONKEYS.

Subdivisions:—Different classes are illustrated by chimpanzee, gorilla, orang-outang and spider monkey. Study shape of the body; feet all like hands, hence such animals are called quadrumanous or four-handed. Body is not well adapted to upright position; this is not the natural posture of a monkey. Ref. ch. 3.

---

*These lectures are pursued from the "First Book of Nature," M. I. Series, by J. E. Talmage.

Self-review:—1. Name some of the peculiarities of the feet of monkeys. 2. Describe a monkey's natural position in walking. 3. State what you know about the gorilla. 4. Describe the orang-outang. 5. Describe the chimpanzee.

Lecture 4.

INSECTIVOROUS ANIMALS OR INSECT-EATERS.

Subdivisions:—Study their use to man. The bat, why not to be called a bird; how the bat catches its prey. The mole, how it makes its underground home. Ref. ch. 4.

Self-review:—1. What are insectivorous animals? Give all the illustrations with which you are acquainted. 2. Describe the bat: showing why it should not be classified with the birds. 3. Describe the bat's method of capturing its prey. 4. Describe the common mole and its home. 5. State what you know of shrews.

Lecture 5.

CARNIVOROUS ANIMALS OR FLESH-EATERS.

Subdivisions:—1. Cat family, including the domestic cat, wild cat, jaguar, leopard, panther, tiger and lion; 2. Dog family—dog, wolf, fox, hyena; 3. Weasel family—weasel, otter, skunk, mink, sable; 4. Bear family—bear, racoon. Study the long claws and sharp teeth of all flesh-eating animals. Ref. ch. 5.

Self-review:—1. Name, with illustrations, the principal families of carnivorous animals. 2. What are the essential differences between the dog family and the cat family of animals? 3. Describe the largest animal of the cat family with which you are acquainted. 4. Describe the weasel. 5. State what you know of each of the principal species of bear.

Lecture 6.

HERBIVOROUS ANIMALS OR PLANT-EATERS.

Subdivisions:—1.—Horse family—horse, donkey, zebra; 2. Ox family, sometimes called Cud-chewers or Ruminants—ox, deer, sheep, camel, giraffe; 3. The Elephant family—Rodent or Gnawing Animals: Mice and rats; gophers; beavers; squirrels, prairie dogs. Ref. chs. 6, 7.

Self-review:—1. Point out the chief differences between the carnivorous and herbivorous animals. 2. Name the common members of the horse family of animals. 3. Describe the digestive organs of a ruminant. 4. State what you have learned about elephants. 5. Describe the rodents, naming all members of the family with which you are acquainted.

LECTURE 7.

BIRDS.

Subdivisions:—Birds: Shape of birds' body; hollow bones; how the bird digests its food; feathers; birds' nests. Kinds of Birds: Birds of Prey: vultures, eagles, hawks, owls. Climbing Birds: wood-peckers, parrots. Scratching Birds: pigeons, domestic fowls. Running Birds: ostrich. Perching Birds: humming birds; mocking birds. Water Birds: waders and swimmers. Ref. chs. 8, 10, 11, 12, 13.

Self-review:—1. Describe the digestive organs of a bird. 2. Show the admirable adaption of the bird's body for flight. 3. Name the principal classes of birds, with illustrations to each. 4. State what you know about birds of prey; climbing birds; scratching birds; running birds; perching birds; water birds. 5. Describe the various kinds of birds' nests with which you are acquainted.

LECTURE 8.

REPTILES.

Subdivisions:—Reptiles: Turtles, snakes; difference between venomous and non-venomous serpents; how to treat a snake bite. Lizards, horned-toads, chameleons, crocodiles and alligators. Ref. chs. 14, 15.

Self-review:—**1.** What is a reptile? 2. State what you know about turtles. 3. Describe each of the principal kinds of snakes with which you are acquainted. 4. How would you treat a person suffering from the bite of a venomous snake? 5. Describe crocodiles and alligators.

LECTURE 9.

AMPHIBIANS AND FISHES.

Subdivisions:—Animals that live partly in air and partly in water. Toads and frogs; the young are called tadpoles. Fishes: shape of the body; how they breathe. Ref. chs. 16, 17, 18.

Self-review:—1. Describe the growth of a frog from the egg to the adult form. 2. State what you know about tree frogs. 3. Describe the fish's body, showing how it is adapted to its watery home. 4. Explain how fishes breathe. 5. Describe the principal kinds of fish with which you are acquainted.

LECTURE 10.

INSECTS.

Subdivisions:—How they grow; egg stage: larva stage: pupa stage; imago stage. Bees and wasps, ants, grasshoppers, butterflies, mosquitoes, flies and beetles, spiders. Ref. chs. 19, 20, 21, 22.

Self-review:—1. Describe the growth of a butterfly from the egg to the winged insect. 2. Describe an insect's compound eye. 3. State what you know of bees and wasps. 4. State what you know about ants and grasshoppers. 5. Describe a spider, showing why spiders are not to be called insects.

LECTURE 11.

WORMS.

. *Subdivisions:*—Land worms, (angle-worms, etc.), water-worms, (leech, etc.); pork-worms, (trichina of pork.) Snails: called mollusks or soft-bodied animals. Sea mollusks: their beautiful shells. Ref. ch. 24.

Self-review:—1. What is a worm? 2. Tell what you know about angle worms. 3. Describe the occurrence of parasitic worms (trichinæ) in the flesh of swine and other animals. 4. What are mollusks? 5. Describe some of the shells of mollusks.

LECTURE 12.

TINY CREATURES.

Subdivisions:—Small animal remains in chalk; how corals live; sponges. What the microscope shows in the water and air. Ref. ch. 25.

Self-review:—1. Describe the structure of chalk, as revealed by the microscope. 2. Describe the amœba. 3. Give illustrations of the abundance of tiny animals in stagnant water, etc. 4. Why are limestone and marble to be considered of animal origin? 5. Why must we not conclude that the larger and more highly developed animals have been produced from the lower forms of animal life?

LECTURE 13.

PLANTS.

Subdivisions:—Their parts: root, stem and branches: leaves; flowers. Root: shape and mode of growth; uses—to support plant in the soil; to absorb nourishment, to store food. Ref. chs. 26, 27.

Self-review:—1. Show the dependence of the animal upon the vegetable kingdom. 2. Show the difference between vegetative and reproductive organs of plants. 3. What are the uses of plant roots? 4. Describe the principal forms of plants roots. 5. Show the difference between annual, biennial and perennial plants.

LECTURE 14.

STEMS AND BRANCHES.

Subdivisions:—Stem consists of bark, woodand pith; difference between heart-wood and sap-wood. Endogenous and exogenous stems. Branches: Parts of stems; tendrils on some climbing plants. Ref. ch. 28.

Self-review:—1. Name and describe the principal parts of a plant stem. 2. Show the difference between exogenous and endogenous stems. 3. What is the difference between heart-wood and sap-wood? 4. What do the rings of plant-growth indicate? 5. Describe the tendrils on some climbing plants.

LECTURE 15.

LEAVES.

Subdivisions:—Shape—simple and compound leaves; parts—petiole, stipules, blades and veins. Uses of leaves—as foliage—to serve as breathing organs. Strange leaves: Pitcher plant; fly-trap leaves, etc. Ref. chs. 29, 30.

Self-review:—1. Examine a typical leaf: describe and name its parts. 2. What is the difference between simple and compound leaves? 3. Explain the uses of leaves to the plants upon which they grow. 4. Describe the common forms of pitcher plants. 5. Describe some fly-catching leaves.

LECTURE 16.

FLOWERS.

Subdivisions:—Parts—calyx, corolla, stamens, pistils. Uses of flowers—essential organs of plant. How flowers are fertilized—by wind; by insects. Ref. chs. 31. 32.

Self-review:—1. Examine a flower; describe and name its parts. 2. What are the uses of flowers to the plants upon which they grow? 3. What is pollen? 4. What is meant by the fertilization of flowers? 5. Explain how the wind and insects are instrumental in fertilizing different flowers.

LECTURE 17.

FRUIT AND SEED.

Subdivisions:—What fruit is—kinds of fruit pod: Berry, prune, gourd. Seed—How the seed sprouts. Experiments in water culture. How seeds travel:—Blown by the wind; dandelion, milkweed, lettuce, thistle, etc. Winged Seeds: Maple, elm, box-elder, ash, pine, etc. Carried by animals; burdock, etc. Ref. chs. 33, 34. *Self-review:*—1. What is the fruit of a plant? 2. Describe fully the pod fruit. 3. Describe with illustrations each of the following kinds of fruit:—gourd, berry, drupe, prune. 4. Describe the germination of a common seed. 5. Explain how some seeds are distributed in nature.

Lecture 18.

PARASITIC PLANTS.

Subdivisions:—How they grow: misletoe, dodder; rust and smut of grain; moulds and mildews. Ref. ch. 35.
Self-review:—1. What is a parasitic plant? 2. Describe the common dodder, and its mode of growth. 3. State what you know of the "potato blight." 4. State what you know about the smut or rust of grain. 5. Describe some common form of mildew or mould.

Lecture 19.

ROCKS AND STONES.

Subdivisions:—How soil is formed; kinds of common stones; siliceous stones; calcareous stones; clay stone; plaster stones. Pebbles: How they are formed and polished; illustrated by the manufacture of boy's marbles, conglomerates or pudding stones. Ref. chs. 36, 37.
Self-review:—1. Briefly describe the formation of soil. 2. Name the principal classes of common stones. 3. How could you distinguish between siliceous and calcareous stones? 4. Explain the formation of pebbles. 5. State what you know about pudding stones.

Lecture 20.

SAND AND MUD.

Subdivisions:—How sand grains are made; sand stones: weathering of rocks; formation of sand dunes; mud, the finest division of rocks. Ref. chs. 38, 39.
Self-review:—1. Explain the formation of sand. 2. Show the difference between fine sand and mud. 3. Explain the effect of wind-driven sand in disintegrating rocks. 4. Explain the

weathering of rocks. 5. Tell what you know of stones formed from mud.

LECTURE 21.
LIMESTONE.

Subdivisions:—Mostly formed from aqueous solutions; purest kinds are marble, calcite, Iceland spar. Limestone formations in caves, stalactites, and stalagmites. Rocks formed by heat. Volcanoes and their effects. Lava flows. Rocky veins; some formed from solutions and others by molten material. Ref. chs. 40, 41, 42.

Self-review:—1. Name the principal kinds of lime carbonates. 2. Explain the agency of coral polyps in producing limestones. 3. Explain and describe calcareous deposits in caves. 4. Explain the formation of aqueous rocks. 5. How are veins formed in rocks?

LECTURE 22.
COAL.

Subdivisions:—Evidences of vegetable origin, coal fossils, ferns, rushes, leaves, fruits. Kinds of coal; anthracite, bituminous coal and lignite. Rocky pictures. How fossils are made; animal and vegetable remains. Rain drop marks; ripple marks. Ref. 43, 44, 45.

Self-review:—1. Why do we believe coal to be of vegetable origin? 2. Describe the principal kinds of coal. 3. What are fossils? 4. Explain the occurrence of rain-marks and ripple-marks in rocks. 5. State what you know of the formation and occurrence of crystals.

LECTURE 23.
THE HEAVENLY BODIES.

Subdivisions:—Grandeur of the heavens by night: how they prove the wisdom and power of a Creator; antiquity of the science of astronomy; appearance of the sky. Ref. ch. 46.

Self-review:—1. What is astronomy? 2. What do you know of the antiquity of this science? 3. What does the telescope teach us concerning the existence of the heavenly bodies in space? 4. Show the difference between the apparent and the real motions of the heavenly bodies. 5. State what you know of the daily motion of the earth.

LECTURE 24.
HEAVENLY BODIES, Continued.

Subdivisions:—The sun. Most brilliant of all the lights of the heavens; supposed size and distance; the earth's orbit about the sun; changes of seasons, sun spots. The moon. The companion planet of the earth; size and distance of the moon; phases or changes of the moon; telescopic appearance of the moon. Why we see but one side of the moon. Eclipses. Eclipses of the sun—caused by moon coming between earth and sun; total, partial and annular eclipses; eclipses of the moon—caused by moon passing into the shadow of the earth; ancient ideas regarding eclipses. Ref. 47, 48.

Self-review:—1. Tell what you know of the supposed size and distance of the sun. 2. Describe the telescopic appearance of the sun. 3. Explain the cause of the seasons. 4. Explain the phases of the moon. 5. Explain the causes of eclipses of the sun and moon.

LECTURE 25.

THE STARS.

Subdivisions:—Two classes to us—fixed stars and planets: planets revolve around sun as does the earth: planets thus far discovered—Mercury, Venus, Earth, Mars, Jupiter, Saturn, Uranus, Neptune; fixed stars innumerable. Ref. ch. 49.

Self-review:—1. What is the difference between fixed stars and planets? 2. Why do the planets sometimes seem as morning stars, and at other times as evening stars? 3. State what you know of the earth as one of the planets. 4. Name in their order of increasing distance from the sun, the planets of our solar system. 5. State what you know of the supposed distance and numbers of the fixed stars.

CIVIL GOVERNMENT.*

WHAT CIVIL GOVERNMENT IS.

Subdivisions:—Definition—Forms of Government—1. Patriarchal--2. Theocratic—3. Monarchial—4. Aristocratic—5. Democratic—6. Republican. Ref. ch. 1 of text-book; including political maxims and review questions.

Self-review:—1. What does government mean? 2. Name the six forms of government. 3. What is the distinction between a Theocratic and an Aristocratic form of government? 4. Give an illustration of a Monarchial form of government. 5. Why is the Patriarchal form of government the basis of all good government? 6. Recite the first five of the political maxims (p. 10).

LESSON 2.

COLONIAL GOVERNMENT.

Subdivisions:—Definition—Settlement of America—Growth of the Colonies. Ref. ch. 2.

Self-review:—1. What is a colony? 2. From what does a colony take its name? 3. Why did the people leave the old country for the new? 4. How long did the British government maintain supremacy over the American colonies? 5. What is meant by the Declaration of Independence? 6. When was the Declaration of Independence made? 7. What was proclaimed in the Declaration? 8. What followed the Declaration? 9. What was the result of the war of Independence? 10. When was peace proclaimed between the two countries?

LESSON 3.

THE ARTICLES OF CONFEDERATION.

Subdivisions:—Declaration of Independence—The Nation—Congress—Articles—Ratification. Ref. ch. 3.

Self-review:-- 1. What was done after the Declaration of Independence? 2. What plan was proposed for the formation of our

---

*This study is pursued from "Townsend's Shorter Course in Civil Government," M. I Course, (See p. 13.); and the "M. I. Diagram and analysis of the Constitution of the United States," by Milton H. Hardy and Geo H. Brimhall.

Rem. For organization of class, see "Instructions to Presidents," pages 12 and 13.

Nation. 3. When did the states ratify the Articles of Confederation? 4. How were the states united during the war for Independence? 5. What were some of the peculiarities of the Articles of Confederation?

Lesson 4.

ORIGIN OF THE CONSTITUTION.

Subdivisions:—Definition—Resolutions—Report of Committee —The Madison Papers—The first Constitutional Congress. Ref. ch. 4.

Self-review:—1. What is meant by the "Constitution of the United States?" 2. What was the Philadelphia Convention? 3. What was the object of this Convention? 4. When did the Committee organize and formally proceed to business? 5. What length of time did the committee continue to hold daily sessions? 6. What is the record of the proceedings of the Convention called? 7. What was the result of the labors of this committee?

Lesson 5.

THE ORIGINAL CONSTITUTION OF THE UNITED STATES OF AMERICA.

Subdivisions:—Preamble—Congress—Senate—House of Representatives—Powers. Ref. first part of ch. 5.

Self-review:—1. What is meant by a preamble? 2. How many reasons are set forth in the preamble for the establishment of the Constitution? 3. Name these reasons in their order. 4. Into how many articles is the original Constitution divided? 5. By reference to the M. I. Diagram and Analysis of the Constitution of the United States, show how the President of the United States is related to the citizen.

Lesson 6.

AMENDMENTS TO THE CONSTITUTION.

Subdivisions:—Nature—Number—Chronology. Ref. last part of ch. 5, including last eight review questions.

Self-review:—1. How many amendments to the Constitution have been adopted? 2. When were the first ten articles declared to be a part of the Constitution? 3. What are the grammatical divisions of the Constitution and its amendments? 4. How many articles? 5. How many sections?

Lesson 7.
THE BRANCHES OF GOVERNMENT.

Subdivisions:—Explanation—Legislative—Executive—Judicial. Ref. ch. 6.

Self-review:—1. What is meant by the constitution of a country? 2. What are the branches of free governments? 3. In whom are these branches respectively vested in the United States? 4. What is the distribution of governmental powers? 5. What is intended by the practical separation of the branches or powers of government? 6. What is the aim of the Constitution with respect to official independence? 7. What is the theory of our government in regard to representation? 8. How is hasty legislation prevented?

Lesson 8.
THE PREAMBLE TO THE CONSTITUTION OF THE UNITED STATES.

Subdivisions:—To form a more perfect union—To establish justice—To insure domestic tranquility—To provide for common defense—To promote the general welfare—To secure the blessings of liberty to ourselves and our posterity. Ref. ch. 7, complete.

Self-review:—1. What is the preamble to the Constitution? 2. What does the preamble set forth? 3. What were the more prominent defects of the Union at the time of the formation of the Constitution as given by an eminent jurist? 4. What is the first object expressed in the preamble? 5. What is the second object mentioned in the preamble? 6. Mention the third object referred to by the preamble. 7. What is the fourth object mentioned in the preamble? 8. What is the fifth object set forth in the preamble? 9. What is the sixth object expressed in the preamble? 10. Recite the preamble.

Lesson 9.
CONGRESS.

Subdivisions:—House of Representatives—Senate. Ref. ch. 8.

Self-review—1. What is the Congress of the U. S.? 2. Of what does it consist? 3. What powers are vested in Congress? 4. How often and when shall Congress assemble? 5. What is the special character of the House of Representatives? 6. How often do we have a new House? 7. What is the Senate? 8. How are Congresses numbered? 9. To what may Congress be compared? 10. What is the relative power of the states in the Senate?

LESSON 10.
HOUSE OF REPRESENTATIVES.

Subdivisions:—How composed—Eligibility—Number of members—Apportionment—Enumeration—By whom elected—Qualification of electors—When elected—Vacancies—Powers. Ref. ch. 9, complete.

Self-review:—1. Draw a diagram of this subject by reference to the *M. I. Diagram* and "Analysis of the Constitution of the U. S." 2. What is the House of Representatives? 3. Why are the members of the House called Representatives? 4. What are the conditions of eligibility to the House? 5. What does the word citizen mean? 6. How can a person become a citizen of the U. S.? 7. What is meant by naturalization? 8. Under whose control was the naturalization before the adoption of the Constitution? 9. State the language of the Constitution regarding the number of representatives. 10. What is the present number of representatives, and how are they apportioned among the states? 11. What are *members at large,* and how are they elected? 12. What is the object of census taking? 13. How are the House powers divided and sub-divided? 14. What bills must originate in the House? 15. What is impeachment?

LESSON 11.
THE SENATE.

Subdivisions:—How composed—By whom chosen—When chosen—How classed—Vacancies—Vote—Presiding officer—Powers. Ref. ch. 10, complete.

Self-review:—How is the Senate of the U. S. composed? 2. Of what is the composition of the Senate the result? 3. What are the conditions of eligibility to the Senate? 4. In what respect are the duties of a senator more responsible than those of a member of the House? 5. What is a senatorial term? 6. By whom are the senators chosen? 7. Why do legislatures claim the right to instruct senators? 8. How long does the Senate exist? 9. Who is the presiding officer of the Senate? 10. What is a treaty? 11. What officers has the Senate? 12. What is the judicial power of the Senate? 13. Diagram this subject, as in lesson 10.

LESSON 12.
PROVISIONS COMMON TO BOTH HOUSES OF CONGRESS.

Subdivisions:—Membership—Ineligibility—Business quorum—

Parliamentary rules—Yeas and nays -Journal—Penalties—Prohibitions—Official oath—Salaries—Official privileges. Ref. ch. 11.

Self-review:—1. What are the conditions of ineligibility? 2.
What constitutes a business quorum in Congress? 3. What provision is made for parliamentary rules? 4. What is the usual
method of taking votes in Congress? 5. What special object is
accomplished by the "yea and nay" method? 6. What special
direction is given in regard to keeping a journal? 7. What provisions are made for penalties? 8. How may a member of Congress
be expelled? 9. What is the distinction between an oath and an
affirmation? 10. On what does the duration of a Congress depend?
11. What are the Constitutional prohibitions on members? 12.
From what are members of Congress privileged? 13. What are
the salaries of Congressmen?

LESSON 13.

POWERS OF CONGRESS.

Subdivisions:—Finances - Commerce—Penalties—Postal — Patent and copyright. Ref. ch. 12. (Pp.110-127.)

Self-review:—1. What are the financial resources of the U. S.
government? 2. What are duties, imposts and excises? 3. What
is the result of fraudulent invoices? 4. What is the first duty of
every government? 5. With whom has Congress power to regulate
commerce? 6. What is money? 7. Why should Congress regulate
the coinage of money? 8. What are the high seas? 9. What is
treason? 10. What is a post road? 11. How may a copyright be
secured? 12. How do patent rights benefit the nation as well as the
inventor? 13. Suggest a limit to patents.

LESSON 14.

POWERS OF CONGRESS.—Continued.

Subdivisions: — War — Judiciary—Naturalization—Territory—
States—Executive vacancy—Appointments—Constitutional amendments—Slavery—General law-making—Meeting. Ref. ch. 12, concluded. (Pp. 129-147.)

Self-review:—1. How is a declaration of war made? 2. What
are letters of marque and reprisal? 3. Explain our militia system.
4. What are the necessary steps of naturalization? 5. How does
the naturalization of the father affect the citizenship of his
sons? 6. How came the U. S. in possession of its present vast

territory? 7. What power has Congress over the state election of its members?

LESSON 15.

LAW-MAKING.

Subdivisions:—First process—Second process—Third process—Orders, Resolutions and votes. Ref. ch. 13.

Self-review:—1. What is a bill? 2. What are the three processes by which bills may become laws? 3. By whom is a bill generally introduced? 4. What may be the effect of a veto? 5. What does the Constitution say in regard to orders, resolutions and vetoes?

LESSON 16.

RESTRICTIONS OF THE POWERS OF THE GENERAL OR NATIONAL GOVERNMENT.

Subdivisions:—Habeas Corpus—Export Duties—Inter-state Commerce—Public Money—Nobility—Penalties—Foreign Slave-trade—Repudiation—Freedom. Ref. ch. 14. complete.

Self-review:—1. Explain a writ of Habeas Corpus. 2. What special privilege is guaranteed by this writ? 3. What restriction is placed by the Constitution in regard to the disbursement of public money? 4. What does the Constitution say of titles of nobility? 5. Explain a bill of attainder and ex-post facto laws. 6. What is meant by repudiation? 7. Why is repudiation enjoined? 8. What does the Constitution provide respecting *Religious Freedom?* 9. How is the freedom of speech, and of the press, and the right to petition provided for? 10. Why is the right to bear arms Constitutionally provided for?

LESSON 17.

RIGHTS OF STATES.

Subdivisions:—Representation—Privilege of Citizenship—State Amity—New States—Election—Militia—Federal Protection—Fugitives—Reservations. Ref. ch. 15, complete.

Self-review:—1. On what does the number of Representatives from any State depend? 2. How is the Senate composed? 3. Why can not the senatorial representation be changed? 4. What provision is made for all the states respecting citizenship? 5. Explain how Virginia was divided notwithstanding the dismemberment clause? 6. What form of government is guaranteed to

each state? 7. What does the Constitution say in regard to
Federal protection? 8. How are the states restricted as to war?
9. What steps must be taken to secure the return of fugitives from
justice? 10. What special rights are reserved to the states. 11.
What does a power conferred imply?

Lesson 18.

STATE SUBORDINATION.

Subdivisions:—State obligations—Supremacy of United States
authority—Official oath. Ref ch. 16.

Self-review:—1. Of how many states was assent to the Constitution necessary to form the Union? 2. What is the origin of state
obligation to the Federal Union? 3. Had the states not ratified
the Constitution what would have been their condition? 4. What
clause of the Constitution establishes the supremacy of the U. S.
authority? 5. What would be the result if the state authority was
supreme? 6. The assent of how many states would be required
today to amend the Constitution?

Lesson 19.

STATE PROHIBITIONS.

Subdivisions:—State relations—Commercial—War—Penalties—
Nobility—Duties. Ref. ch. 17.

Self-review:—1. Why is it unsafe to vest the states with treaty
power? 2. What commercial power are the states forbidden to
exercise? 3. What are bills of credit? 4. What is currency? 5.
What restrictions are placed on the states in regard to money
tender? 6. Under what circumstances may a state raise troops
without the consent of Congress? 7. What are the state prohibitions in regard to bills of attainder, and ex-post facto laws? 8.
What are the restrictions about exports and imports? 9. What is
the object of inspection laws? 10. To what must the provisions of
all state constitutions conform?

Lesson 20.

PERSONAL RIGHTS.

Subdivisions:—Domicile — Search and Seizures — Judicial —
Criminal actions—Civil actions—Treason. Ref. ch. 18.

Self-review:—1. What does the Constitution say about quarter-
ing soldiers in private houses? 2. What is said about unreasonable
searches and seizures? 3. What conditions are necessary to the

issue of warrants? 4. Recite the fifth article of the amendments to the Constitution. 5. Why can a person not be tried twice for the same offense? 6. What is the first object of government? 7. What is the distinction between a grand jury and a petit jury? 8. Explain *bail* and *fines*. 9. When and by whom was jury trial established in England? 10. In what cases may a trial by jury be claimed? 11. Recite the sixth article of amendments to the Constitution.

LESSON 21.

THE EXECUTIVE. (Prest. U.S.)

Subdivisions:—In whom vested—Executive term—Eligibility—How elected—Oath of office—How removable—Salary—Powers and duties. Ref. ch. 19.

Self-review:—1. In whom is the executive power vested? 2. In whom was it vested under the confederation? 3. What are the conditions of eligibility to the office of President of the United States? 4. Describe the two methods by which the President may be elected. 5. What is the President's oath of office? 6. How is the President removable? 7. What is the salary of the President? 8. What is furnished besides his salary? 9. What is the military authority of the President? 10. Explain the power of reprieve and pardon. 11. What control has the President over appointments? 12. What is an ambassador, a consul, a minister? 13. What has the President to do with the Judges of the Supreme Court? 14. What authority is given the President in regard to the convening and adjourning of Congress? 15. What if the President should decline to execute the laws? 16. What is a commission? 17. Who commissions the officers of the U. S.?

LESSON 22.

THE EXECUTIVE, Continued. (V. Prest.)

Subdivisions:—Eligibility—Election—Oath of office--Term of office—Powers and duties. Ref. ch. 20.

Self-review:—1. To what office must the Vice-President be eligible? 2. What are the three conditions of eligibility? 3. In which instances has the Vice-President been called to the Presidential office? 4. In what two ways may the Vice-President be elected? 5. What are the powers and duties of the Vice-President? 6. Wherein do the duties of the Vice-President differ from those of the speaker of the house? 7. What is the title of the Vice-President when the duties of the President devolve upon him?

LESSON 23.

JUDICIARY.

Subdivisions: —Where vested—Judges—Jurisdiction. Ref. ch. 21.

Self-review:—1. What is said of a government having a feeble judiciary? 2. What kind of courts were under the Confederation? 3. Where is the judicial power vested now? 4. What is the Supreme Court of the United States? 5. How many Judges of the Supreme Court? 6. How is the United States divided judicially? 7. Name the various U. S. Courts. 8. By whom are the Judges of the Supreme Court appointed? 9. What is meant by judicial power? 10. Explain the terms "Law," "Equity," and "Jurisdiction." 11. Where are controversies to be tried to which the U. S. is a party?

LESSON 24.

GENERAL VIEW OF THE GOVERNMENT OF UTAH.

Subdivisions:—Form of government—When organized—Legislative Department—Executive—Judiciary. Ref. Organic Act, Laws of Utah.

Self-review:—1. What form of government is provided for Utah? 2. What is the Organic Act? 3. When was the Territory organized? 4. Of what does the law-making department consist? 5. In whom is the executive power vested? 6. Name the governors of Utah to date. 7. What is the chief distinction between a state and a territorial government? 8. Explain the county divisions and name the counties of Utah. 9. Explain the distinction between the County Court, the Probate Court, and the District Court.

LESSON 25.

CITY, TOWN AND PRECINCT.

Subdivisions:—City Charter—Departments of city government —Relationship of city ordinances to state or territorial statutes— Town Organizations—Organization of precincts—Precinct officers.

Self-review:—1. Draw up a complete diagram of the government of your locality. 2. Name the officers of a precinct. 3. What steps should a community take to effect a town organization? 4. What are the advantages of a municipality? 5. What form of government must be guaranteed to every citizen of every locality in the U. S.?

LITERATURE.

READINGS FROM IRVING.*

---

*The following *ten* descriptions are pursued from "Readings from Washington Irving," M. I. series. The fifteen biographical studies from "Life of Nepbi," M. I. series, make the twenty-five exercises for the year. (See p. 64).

AMERICAN LITERATURE.*

1st Month's Study.

History and early characteristics. Literature of the Pilgrims; Jonathan Edwards; Literature of the Revolution; Patriotic oratory; Hamilton, Adams, Patrick Henry.

2nd Month's Study.

Colonial and Revolutionary Historians. Sullivan, Trumbull, Gayerre, Young, Moultrie, Winthrop, Cheever, Upham, Dr. Ramsay.

3rd Month's Study.

Early American Poetry. Dwight, Humphreys, John Trumbull, Freneau, Joel Barlow.

4th Month's Study.

Early oratory of the present century. Story, Kent, Webster, Choate, Clay, Randolph, Everett.

5th Month's Study.

Development of History and Biography. Bancroft, Prescott, Motley, Irving, Hildreth, Cooper, Lossing.

6th Month's Study.

Later American Poets and Poetry. Writings of Longfellow, Bryant, Whittier, Poe, Holmes, Lowell, Saxe, Bayard Taylor.

7th Month's Study.

The essayists: Irving, Emerson, Dr. Channing, Mitchell, Dr. Holland. E. P. Whipple, W. D. Howells, Gail Hamilton.

*For reference see "Manual of American Literature," by N. K. Royse, and "Richardson's American Literature," (Popular Edition).

SUGGESTIONS.

Besides the indispensable text-books for the regular course mentioned under head of "Instructions to Members," p. 14, and the books referred to in the Church History Subjects, pp. 49 to 56, Bible History, pp. 24 to 31, and Book of Mormon History, pp. 32 to 40, the students will find it greatly to their advantage to have access through their private or public libraries to the following suggestive additional books for reference in pursuing the course outlined in this Manual, and especially for the advanced classes or sections:

Ready Reference.
Prescott's Conquest of Mexico.
Stephens' and Catherwood's Travels in Yucatan.
Voices from Babylon.
History of Utah.
Eggleston's History of the United States.
Townsend's Analysis of Civil Government.
Tenney's Natural History of Animals.
Hooker's Geology.
Steele's Zoology.
Newcomb and Holden's or Ray's Astronomy.
Webster's Unabridged Dictionary (International).
Shaw's English Literature.
Swinton's Literary Reader.
Day's Introduction to English Literature.
And some popular Cyclopædia.

www.ingramcontent.com/pod-product-compliance
Lightning Source LLC
Chambersburg PA
CBHW021420090426
42742CB00009B/1196